Presented to

_____

On the occasion of

_____

From

_____

Date

_____

D1359976

TO KNOW GOD

Understanding the Nature of God

A Barbour Book

Published by Barbour & Company, Inc.
       P.O. Box 719
       Uhrichsville, Ohio 44683
       http://www.barbourbooks.com

 Member of the
Evangelical Christian
Publishers Association

Printed in the United States of America.

CONTENTS

Preface

THE BASIC NATURE OF GOD

THE CHARACTER QUALITIES OF GOD

THE ROLES OF GOD

THE SPECIAL ROLES OF JESUS

PREFACE

God is real. God wants to share life with you. God knows you and wants you to know Him. He gave us the Bible so we could know about Him. As we read the Bible and think deeply upon its truths, God will make Himself known to us.

What is the Bible?

The Bible is made up of sixty-six different accounts, letters, and writings that we call the "books" of the Bible. These were written by different godly men at different times and places. However, the Bible is more than just the words of men. As these men wrote, God was working through them to get the exact words that He wanted written. What we have in the Bible are the truths that came from God Himself.

The Old Testament books were originally written in the Hebrew language and the New Testament books were written in the Greek language. Since we don't use these ancient languages, educated men have translated the Bible into the modern versions so that we can read and understand God's Word.

How is the Bible arranged?

The Old Testament books are the accounts of God's first dealings with man. They tell of God's special dealings with a man, Abraham, and his descendants, the Jews, who were the ancestors of Jesus Christ. The New Testament tells the story of Jesus' life and what happened among His followers after He rose from the dead and returned to heaven. Also, it contains letters written by His followers that explain who Jesus is, what He accomplished, and how we can live with Him today.

The books themselves were later broken into chapters, and the chapters into verses, so that readers could more easily locate Scriptures.

Please Note

Words that come directly out of the Bible are shown in *italics*. Words of Jesus are show in *ITALICS SMALL CAPS*.

THE BASIC NATURE OF GOD

GOD
IS SPIRIT

He is not limited to a physical form but exists alongside the physical world.

Jesus said, *GOD IS SPIRIT, AND HIS WORSHIPERS MUST WORSHIP IN SPIRIT AND IN TRUTH.*[1] We must realize that this *God of the spirits of all mankind*[2] *is over all and through all and in all.*[3] Indeed, He is *the King eternal, immortal, invisible*[4] who *lives in unapproachable light, whom no one has seen or can see.*[5]

How can we know this invisible spirit? He sent His son, Jesus, so that we could know Him. *No one has ever seen God, but God the only Son. . .has made him known.*[6] *He is the image of the invisible God.*[7]

In our dead spiritual state we are without God. That is why Jesus said, *UNLESS A MAN IS BORN OF WATER AND THE SPIRIT, HE CANNOT ENTER THE KINGDOM OF GOD. FLESH GIVES BIRTH TO FLESH, BUT THE SPIRIT GIVES BIRTH TO SPIRIT.*[8] Because only *THE SPIRIT GIVES LIFE.*[9]

Yes, *the Lord is the Spirit, and where the Spirit of the Lord is, there is freedom.*[10]

So *he saved us through the washing of rebirth and renewal by the Holy Spirit.*[11] And now *the Spirit himself testifies with our spirit that we are God's children.*[12]

The final evidence that this has happened is the work He does in our lives. As He works in us we see that *the fruit of the Spirit is love, joy, peace, patience, kindness, goodness, faithfulness, gentleness and self-control.*[13]

[1]John 4:24
[2]Numbers 16:22
[3]Ephesians 4:6
[4]1 Timothy 1:17
[5]1 Timothy 6:16
[6]John 1:18
[7]Colossians 1:15
[8]John 3:5,6
[9]John 6:63
[10]2 Corinthians 3:17
[11]Titus 3:5
[12]Romans 8:16
[13]Galatians 5:22,23

GOD IS
ETERNAL

Before any time period that we can imagine, He had always been alive, and He will continue to live forever.

Right from the beginning God is referred to as *the LORD, the Eternal God.*[1] God comes right out and says, *I live forever.*[2] Yes, the LORD is *from all eternity*[3] and *the LORD is King for ever and ever.*[4]

In all respects, *how great is God— beyond our understanding! The number of his years is past finding out.*[5] Because *with the Lord a day is like a thousand years, and a thousand years are like a day.*[6] Truly, *the King eternal, immortal*[7] is the Lord God Almighty, who was, and is, and is to come.*[8]

Since Jesus is God in human form, only He could say things like BEFORE ABRAHAM WAS BORN, I AM.[9] You see, *all things were created by him and for him. He is before all things.*[10] Jesus is *without beginning of days or end of life.*[11]

However, this eternal God *has set eternity in the hearts of men.*[12] God sees this part of us and wants to share His eternal life with us. Jesus said, MY FATHER'S WILL IS THAT EVERYONE WHO LOOKS TO THE SON AND BELIEVES IN HIM SHALL HAVE ETERNAL LIFE.[13]

By knowing God we can have this life. As Jesus stated, *THIS IS ETERNAL LIFE: THAT THEY MAY KNOW YOU, THE ONLY TRUE GOD, AND JESUS CHRIST, WHOM YOU HAVE SENT.*[14] Now we who have received Him can say that *God has given us eternal life, and this life is in his Son. He who has the Son has life.*[15]

[1]Genesis 21:33
[2]Deuteronomy 32:40
[3]Psalm 93:2
[4]Psalm 10:16
[5]Job 36:26
[6]2 Peter 3:8
[7]1 Timothy 1:17
[8]Revelation 4:8
[9]John 8:58
[10]Colossians 1:16-17
[11]Hebrews 7:3
[12]Ecclesiastes 3:11
[13]John 6:40
[14]John 17:3
[15]1 John 5:11,12

GOD IS EVERYWHERE

He is larger than the universe and He can be at all places at all times.

It is easy to think that God is in a special place or holy building. Actually, *the God who made the world and everything in it is the Lord of heaven and earth and does not live in temples built by hands.[1]* He is so big that *with the breadth of his hand* He *marked off the heavens.[2]* Truly, *the heavens, even the highest heavens, cannot contain him.[3]*

"Do I not fill the heavens and the earth?" declares the LORD.[4] He sees all, for *the eyes of the Lord are everywhere.[5]* He is not a far away God. In fact, *in him we live and move and have our being.[6]*

By faith I can now say, *If I go up to the heavens, you are there; if I make my bed in the depths, you are there. If I rise on the wings of the dawn, if I settle on the far side of the sea, even there your hand will guide me, your right hand will hold me fast.*[7]

During tough times He reminds us, *When you pass through the waters, I will be with you.*[8] Because *my presence will go with you, and I will give you rest.*[9]

Sometimes people turn away from God, but He says, *Never will I leave you; never will I forsake you.*[10] This is not temporary. Jesus tells us, *I AM WITH YOU ALWAYS, TO THE VERY END OF THE AGE.*[11]

The LORD himself goes before you and will be with you; he will never leave you nor forsake you. Do not be afraid; do not be discouraged.[12]

[1]Acts 17:24
[2]Isaiah 40:12
[3]2 Chronicles 2:6
[4]Jeremiah 23:24
[5]Proverbs 15:3
[6]Acts 17:28
[7]Psalm 139:8-10
[8]Isaiah 43:2
[9]Exodus 33:14
[10]Hebrews 13:5
[11]Matthew 28:20
[12]Deuteronomy 31:8

GOD IS ALL-KNOWING

Everything there is to know about things in the past, the present, or in the future has always been known by Him.

The LORD is a God who knows.[1] In reality, *he knows everything*[2] and *his understanding has no limit.*[3] He is so far beyond human intelligence that *his understanding no one can fathom.*[4]

David stated, *You know when I sit and when I rise; you perceive my thoughts from afar. You discern my going out and my lying down; you are familiar with all my ways. Before a word is on my tongue you know it completely, O LORD.*[5]

Now, God is interested in people, so *his eyes are on the ways of men, he* sees their every step.[6] In fact, *the LORD searches every heart and understands every motive behind the thoughts.*[7]

He says to us *I know what is going through your mind.*[8]

It can be uncomfortable to realize that *everything is uncovered and laid bare before the eyes of him to whom we must give account.*[9]

But God is not out to use His knowledge against us. Instead, *the Lord knows those who are his.*[10] This is a knowledge of closeness since *the man who loves God is known by God.*[11]

Therefore, He is always prepared when we pray to Him because *YOUR FATHER KNOWS WHAT YOU NEED BEFORE YOU ASK HIM.*[12] Thus, when we go through trying times we can trust that *he knows*

*the way that I take; when he has tested
me, I will come forth as gold.*[13]

[1]1 Samuel 2:3
[2]1 John 3:20
[3]Psalm 147:5
[4]Isaiah 40:28
[5]Psalm 139:2-4
[6]Job 34:21
[7]1 Chronicles 28:9
[8]Ezekiel 11:5
[9]Hebrews 4:13
[10]2 Timothy 2:19
[11]1 Corinthians 8:3
[12]Matthew 6:8
[13]Job 23:10

GOD IS
ALL-POWERFUL

God is not restrained or controlled by anything other than Himself, and He does all He wants to do without tiring Himself.

"I am the Alpha and the Omega," says the Lord God, *"who is, and who was, and who is to come, the Almighty."*[1] The angel said to Mary, *nothing is impossible with God.*[2] When discussing difficult things with His followers, Jesus reminded them that *WITH GOD ALL THINGS ARE POSSIBLE.*[3]

Lord, *you can do all things; no plan of yours can be thwarted.*[4] Yes, *our God is in heaven; he does whatever pleases him.*[5] *He will not grow tired or weary.*[6]

To Abraham, the father of believers in God, He said, *I am God Almighty.*[7] This is why Abraham was *fully persuaded that God had power to do what he had promised.*[8] And even though it had not been done before, *Abraham reasoned that God could raise the dead.*[9]

With these things in mind a believer can say, *I know whom I have believed, and am convinced that he is able to guard what I have entrusted to him.*[10]

We trust that He will strengthen us because *God is able to make all grace abound to you, so that in all things at all times, having all that you need, you will abound in every good work.*[11]

Indeed, we know we are protected as His own since Jesus said to His followers, *MY FATHER, WHO HAS GIVEN THEM (my sheep) TO ME, IS GREATER THAN ALL;*

*NO ONE CAN SNATCH THEM OUT OF MY
FATHER'S HAND.*[12]

[1]Revelation 1:8
[2]Luke 1:37
[3]Matthew 19:26
[4]Job 42:2
[5]Psalm 115:3
[6]Isaiah 40:28
[7]Genesis 17:1
[8]Romans 4:21
[9]Hebrews 11:19
[10]2 Timothy 1:12
[11]2 Corinthians 9:8
[12]John 10:29

God Is Unique

Because He is infinitely greater than any other thing or being, there is only one of Him and none like Him.

See now that I myself am he! There is no god besides me.[1] Before me no god was formed, nor will there be one after me.[2] I am the first and I am the last; apart from me there is no God.[3]

I have not spoken in secret. . .I have not said "Seek me in vain". . .Ignorant are those who carry about idols of wood, who pray to gods that cannot save. . . Turn to me and be saved, all you ends of the earth; for I am God, and there is no other.[4]

The LORD is God in heaven above

and on the earth below. There is no other.⁵ There is. . .one God and Father of all.⁶

There is one God and one mediator between God and men, the man Christ Jesus.⁷

For even if there are so-called gods, whether in heaven or on earth (as indeed there are many "gods" and many "lords"), yet for us there is but one God, the Father, from whom all things came and for whom we live; and there is but one Lord, Jesus Christ, through whom all things came and through whom we live.⁸

How great you are, O Sovereign LORD! There is no one like you, and there is no God but you.⁹ NOW THIS IS ETERNAL LIFE: THAT THEY MAY KNOW YOU, THE ONLY TRUE GOD, AND JESUS CHRIST, WHOM YOU HAVE SENT.¹⁰

[1]Deuteronomy 32:39
[2]Isaiah 43:10
[3]Isaiah 44:6
[4]Isaiah 45:19-20,22
[5] Deuteronomy 4:39
[6]Ephesians 4:6
[7]1 Timothy 2:5
[8]1 Corinthians 8:5-6
[9]2 Samuel 7:22
[10]John 17:3

GOD IS
PERFECT

There is nothing about Him that could be improved or corrected; He never errs or does wrong.

Can anyone teach knowledge to God?[1] It is hard to imagine someone who is perfect just the way He is. We always make mistakes, but *as for God, his way is perfect; the word of the LORD is flawless.*[2] Because *he is the Rock, his works are perfect, and all his ways are just. A faithful God who does no wrong, upright and just is he.*[3]

Nothing about Him is "new and improved," for *everything God does will endure forever; nothing can be added to it and nothing taken from it.*[4] Put simply, *YOUR HEAVENLY FATHER IS PERFECT.*[5]

God might seem far from ones so imperfect as us. Indeed, *all have sinned and fall short of the glory of God.*[6] However, Jesus bridged the gap between God and men. He is the one *mediator between God and man.*[7]

First, God wipes out our record of past wrong: *By one sacrifice he has made perfect forever those who are being made holy.*[8]

Then He works in us to make us right: *It is God who arms me with strength and makes my way perfect.*[9]

Finally, He prepares a way to bring us into His perfection: *He has reconciled you by Christ's physical body through death to present you holy in his sight, without blemish and free from accusation.*[10]

Sometimes this comes through hardship but *the God of all grace, who called you to his eternal glory in Christ, after you have suffered a little while, will himself restore you and make you strong, firm, and steadfast.*[11]

[1]Job 21:22
[2]Psalm 18:30
[3]Deuteronomy 32:4
[4]Ecclesiastes 3:14
[5]Matthew 5:48
[6]Romans 3:23
[7]1 Timothy 2:5
[8]Hebrews 10:14
[9]Psalm 18:32
[10]Colossians 1:22
[11]1 Peter 5:10

God Is Unchanging

Because He is perfect, all-knowing, and all-powerful, He is not subject to change, growth, or adjustment.

I the LORD do not change.[1] This sets Him apart from the world that we know. *In the beginning you laid the foundations of the earth, and the heavens are the work of your hands. They will perish, but you remain; they will all wear out like a garment. Like clothing you will change them and they will be discarded. But you remain the same, and your years will never end.*[2]

His nature does not change and His good character does not change either. *Every good and perfect gift is from above, coming down from the Father of the heavenly lights, who does not change like shifting shadows.*[3]

This also applies to our Savior, God's Son. *Jesus Christ is the same yesterday and today and forever.*[4]

God is not a man, that he should lie, nor a son of man, that he should change his mind. Does he speak and then not act? Does he promise and not fulfill?[5] So, *it is better to take refuge in the LORD than to trust in man.*[6]

God, who has called you into fellowship with his Son Jesus Christ our Lord, is faithful.[7] When he says something, we can rely on it. *Not one word has failed of all the good promises he gave.*[8]

You see, *because God wanted to make the unchanging nature of his purpose very clear to the heirs of what was*

promised, he confirmed it with an oath.
God did this so that, by two unchange-
able things in which it is impossible for
God to lie, we who have fled to take hold
of the hope offered to us may be greatly
encouraged.[9]

[1]Malachi 3:6
[2]Psalm 102:25-27
[3]James 1:17
[4]Hebrews 13:8
[5]Numbers 23:19
[6]Psalm 118:8
[7]1 Corinthians 1:9
[8]1 Kings 8:56
[9]Hebrews 6:17-18

GOD IS THREE-IN-ONE

Within the one God there are three persons who take on different roles but share the same being.

We see that there are several persons in the one God when He says, *Let us make man in our image.*[1]

God the Father: Moses talked to God's people and he asked, Is *he not your Father, your Creator?*[2] Jesus said, YOU HAVE ONE FATHER, AND HE IS IN HEAVEN.[3]

God the Son: Jesus said, *I AND THE FATHER ARE ONE.*[4] He is *our great God and Savior, Jesus Christ.*[5] Indeed, *the Son is the radiance of God's glory and the exact representation of his being.*[6]

God the Holy Spirit: *The Lord is the Spirit.[7]* This is brought out by Peter when he confronts some dishonest people. First he says, *you have lied to the Holy Spirit,[8]* and then he states, *you have not lied to men but to God.[8]*

Each is given equal status when Jesus says to baptize *IN THE NAME OF THE FATHER AND OF THE SON AND OF THE HOLY SPIRIT.[9]*

The Father, in love, initiates our salvation. *How great is the love the Father has lavished on us,[10]* for *he sent his one and only Son into the world that we might live through him.[11]*

The Son, Jesus, accomplishes the acts which bring us grace. *Christ died for sins once for all, the righteous for the unrighteous, to bring you to God.[12]*

The Spirit does the work in us. *THE*

HOLY SPIRIT, WHOM THE FATHER WILL SEND IN MY NAME, WILL TEACH YOU ALL THINGS.[13]

When we meet the three-in-one God we can live in *the grace of the Lord Jesus Christ, and the love of God, and the fellowship of the Holy Spirit.*[14]

[1]Genesis 1:26
[2]Deuteronomy 32:6
[3]Matthew 23:9
[4]John 10:30
[5]Titus 2:13
[6]Hebrews 1:3
[7]2 Corinthians 3:17
[8]Acts 5:3,4
[9]Matthew 28:19
[10]1 John 3:1
[11]1 John 4:9
[12]1 Peter 3:18
[13]John 14:26
[14]2 Corinthians 13:14

God Is Glorious

His special nature brings forth wonder, praise, and respect from all who know Him.

The LORD Almighty—he is the King of glory.[1] The God of glory[2] is majestic in holiness, awesome in glory.[3]

God's glory has been unveiled in various ways: To all men *the heavens declare the glory of God; the skies proclaim the work of his hands.[4]* But, *to the Israelites the glory of the LORD looked like a consuming fire on top of the mountain.[5]*

The prophet said that *the glory of the LORD will be revealed.[6]* This was done in Jesus. At Jesus' birth there were shepherds nearby, and *the glory of the Lord shone around them.*[7] His follower, Peter, said, *we were eyewitnesses of his majesty.*[8] And His disciple, John, added, *we have seen his glory, the glory of the one and only Son, who came from the Father, full of grace and truth.*[9]

The good news is that *when Christ, who is your life, appears, then you also will appear with him in glory.*[10] This is possible because Jesus *will transform our lowly bodies so that they will be like his glorious body.*[11] Jesus even said that *THE RIGHTEOUS WILL SHINE LIKE THE SUN IN THE KINGDOM OF THEIR FATHER.*[12]

We can have hope when we keep in mind that *our light and momentary troubles are achieving for us an eternal glory that far outweighs them all.*[13]

Then we can say to the Lord in faith,

you guide me with your counsel and afterward you will take me into glory.[14]

[1]Psalm 24:10
[2]Acts 7:2
[3]Exodus 15:11
[4]Psalm 19:1
[5]Exodus 24:17
[6]Isaiah 40:5
[7]Luke 2:9
[8]2 Peter 1:16
[9]John 1:14
[10]Colossians 3:4
[11]Philippians 3:21
[12]Matthew 13:43
[13]2 Corinthians 4:17
[14]Psalm 73:24

GOD IS MORAL

He has values and He sets values that apply throughout all creation and time.

The LORD is righteous, he loves justice.[1] God is not some neutral Being. He said, *I am the LORD, who exercises kindness, justice and righteousness on earth, for in these I delight.*[2]

He not only loves right ways but *there are six things the LORD hates, seven that are detestable to him: haughty eyes, a lying tongue, hands that shed innocent blood, a heart that devises wicked schemes, feet that are quick to rush into evil, a false witness who pours out lies, and a man who stirs up dissension among brothers.*[3]

He is *the Lord, the Lord, the compassionate and gracious God, slow to anger, abounding in love and faithfulness, maintaining love to thousands, and forgiving wickedness, rebellion and sin. Yet he does not leave the guilty unpunished.*[4] He is willing to forgive but also ready to punish.

In days when everyone does what they feel is right for them, we need to remember that *the ways of the Lord are right; the righteous walk in them, but the rebellious stumble in them.*[5]

God's law and ways are not without purpose. They not only please God but they have good results in the lives of those who follow them. *The law of the Lord is perfect, reviving the soul. The statutes of the Lord are trustworthy, making wise the simple. The precepts of the Lord are right, giving joy to the heart. The commands of the LORD are radiant, giving light to the eyes. They are more precious than gold, than much pure gold; they are sweeter than honey, than honey from the comb. By them is your servant warned; in keeping them there is great reward.*[6]

[1]Psalm 11:7
[2]Jeremiah 9:24
[3]Proverbs 6:16-19
[4]Exodus 34:6,7
[5]Hosea 14:9
[6]Psalm 19:7-8,10-11

GOD IS PERSONAL

He makes Himself known, and He seeks to share His life with people.

God wanted to share life with someone. He said, *Let us make man in our image, in our likeness.[1]* He repeatedly spoke with the first man and woman.[2] And when they broke His rules *they hid from the LORD God among the trees of the garden. But the LORD God called to the man, "Where are you?"[3]*

Since then God has worked in various ways to point people back to Himself. *God did this so that men would seek him and perhaps reach out for him and find him, though he is not far from each one of us.[4]* This is because *the LORD is near to all who call on him, to all who call on him in truth.*[5]

Jesus said, *THE TRUE WORSHIPERS WILL WORSHIP THE FATHER IN SPIRIT AND TRUTH, FOR THEY ARE THE KIND OF WORSHIPERS THE FATHER SEEKS.*[6]

Not only does the Father seek us, but Jesus, *THE SON OF MAN CAME TO SEEK AND TO SAVE WHAT WAS LOST.*[7]

When we finally find God we discover that He was finding us. He says to us, *I have loved you with an everlasting love; I have drawn you with loving-kindness.*[8] So, *come near to God and he will come near to you.*[9]

Yes, *let us draw near to God with a sincere heart in full assurance of faith.*[10]

And *let us then approach the throne of grace with confidence, so that we may receive mercy and find grace to help us in our time of need.*[11]

[1]Genesis 1:26
[2]Genesis 1,2,3
[3]Genesis 3:8
[4]Acts 17:27
[5]Psalm 145:18
[6]John 4:23
[7]Luke 19:10
[8]Jeremiah 31:3
[9]James 4:8
[10]Hebrews 10:22
[11]Hebrews 4:16

NOTES

_____

_____

_____

_____

_____

_____

_____

_____

_____

_____

_____

_____

_____

_____

_____

_____

_____

NOTES

_____

_____

_____

_____

_____

_____

_____

_____

_____

_____

_____

_____

_____

_____

_____

_____

THE
CHARACTER
QUALITIES
OF
GOD

GOD IS COMPASSIONATE

He feels the hurts that people have and He wants to help them.

The LORD is compassionate and gracious, slow to anger, abounding in love.[1] Actually, He calls Himself *"The LORD, the LORD, the compassionate and gracious God".[2]* Yes, *our God is full of compassion.[3]*

Because of the LORD's great love we are not consumed, for his compassions never fail. They are new every morning.[4] As a father has compassion on his children, so the LORD has compassion on those who fear him.[5]

For this is what the high and lofty One says—he who lives forever, whose name is holy: *"I live in a high and holy place, but also with him who is contrite and lowly in spirit, to revive the spirit of the lowly and to revive the heart of the contrite.*[6]

When he saw the crowds, he had compassion on them, because they were harassed and helpless, like sheep without a shepherd.[7] *In all their distress he too was distressed.*[8]

We do not have a high priest (Jesus) *who is unable to sympathize with our weaknesses, but we have one who has been tempted in every way, just as we are—yet was without sin. Let us then approach the throne of grace with confidence, so that we may receive mercy and find grace to help us in our time of need.*[9]

Praise be to the God and Father of our Lord Jesus Christ, the Father of compassion and the God of all comfort, who comforts us in all our troubles, so that we can comfort those in any trouble with the comfort we ourselves have received from God.[10]

[1]Psalm 103:8
[2]Exodus 34:6
[3]Psalm 116:5
[4]Lamentations 3:22,23
[5]Psalm 103:13
[6]Isaiah 57:15
[7]Matthew 9:36
[8]Isaiah 63:9
[9]Hebrews 4:15,16
[10]2 Corinthians 1:3,4

God Is Faithful

He always does what He promised and He always completes what He started.

The LORD your God is God; he is the faithful God.[1] He is *the faithful Holy One.[2]* David said, *your love, O LORD, reaches to the heavens, your faithfulness to the skies.[3] Your faithfulness surrounds you.[4]*

Not one word has failed of all the good promises he gave.[5] So let us hold unswervingly to the hope we profess, for he who promised is faithful.[6] And those who suffer according to God's will should commit themselves to their faithful Creator.[7]

He who began a good work in you

will carry it on to completion until the day of Christ Jesus.[8] God is faithful; he will not let you be tempted beyond what you can bear.[9] He will keep you strong to the end, so that you will be blameless on the day of our Lord Jesus Christ. God, who has called you into fellowship with his Son Jesus Christ Our Lord, is faithful.[10]

Even to your old age and gray hairs I am he, I am he who will sustain you. I have made you and I will carry you; I will sustain you and I will rescue you.[11] Can a mother forget the baby at her breast and have no compassion on the child she has borne? Though she may forget, I will not forget you! [12]

Though the mountains be shaken and the hills be removed, yet my unfailing love for you will not be shaken.[13] Never will I leave you; never will I forsake you.[14]

May your whole spirit, soul and body be kept blameless at the coming of our Lord Jesus Christ. The one who calls you is faithful and he will do it.[15]

[1]Deuteronomy 7:9
[2]Hosea 11:12
[3]Psalm 36:5
[4]Psalm 89:8
[5]1 Kings 8:56
[6]Hebrews 10:23
[7]1 Peter 4:19
[8]Philippians 1:6
[9]1 Corinthians 10:13
[10]1 Corinthians 1:8,9
[11]Isaiah 46:4
[12]Isaiah 49:15
[13]Isaiah 54:10
[14]Hebrews 13:5
[15]1 Thessalonians 5:23,24

GOD IS FORGIVING

He finds a way to forget our offenses without changing His law.

Who is a God like you, who pardons sin and forgives?. . .You do not stay angry forever but delight to show mercy.[1] Only God is able to change the memory of our sins. *I, even I, am he who blots out your transgressions, for my own sake, and remembers your sins no more.*[2] *Though your sins are like scarlet, they shall be as white as snow.*[3]

Because He *forgives all my sins,*[4] then *he does not treat us as our sins deserve or repay us according to our iniquities.*[5] Instead, *as far as the east is from the west, so far has he removed our transgressions from us.*[6]

Seek the LORD while he may be found; call on him while he is near. Let the wicked forsake his way and the evil man his thoughts. Let him turn to the LORD, and he will have mercy on him, and to our God, for he will freely pardon.[7]

How can this be? Does God let our crimes go unpunished? No, *Christ was sacrificed once to take away the sins of many people.[8] He himself bore our sins in his body on the* (cross).[9] Through Christ *he forgave us all our sins.[10]* And now *through Jesus the forgiveness of sins is proclaimed to you.[11]* Since it does not, therefore, *depend on man's desire or effort, but on God's mercy.[12]*

Believers say to God, *"We do not make requests of you because we are righteous, but because of your great mercy."[13]* We know that *if we confess our sins, he is faithful and just and will for-*

give us our sins and purify us from all unrighteousness.[14] So let us draw near to God with a sincere heart in full assurance of faith, having our hearts sprinkled to cleanse us from a guilty conscience.[15]

[1]Micah 7:18
[2]Isaiah 43:25
[3]Isaiah 1:18
[4]Psalm 103:3
[5]Psalm 103:10
[6]Psalm 103:12
[7]Isaiah 55:6,7
[8]Hebrews 9:28
[9]1 Peter 2:24
[10]Colossians 2:13
[11]Acts 13:38
[12]Romans 9:16
[13]Daniel 9:18
[14]1 John 1:9
[15]Hebrews 10:22

GOD IS GENTLE

He does not force His way on the soul of man; He serves and He speaks with a light touch.

God's gentleness is shown in *the meekness and gentleness of Christ.*[1] When confronted by enemies Jesus said, *DO YOU THINK I CANNOT CALL ON MY FATHER, AND HE WILL AT ONCE PUT AT MY DISPOSAL MORE THAN TWELVE LEGIONS (72,000) OF ANGELS?*[2] However, He chose the gentle way instead. When Jesus rode into Jerusalem it was said, *"See, your king comes to you, gentle and riding on a donkey."*[3]

Christ Jesus: Who, being in very nature God, did not consider equality with God something to be grasped, but made himself nothing, taking the very nature of a servant, being made in human likeness. And being found in appearance as a man, he humbled himself and became obedient to death—even death on a cross![4]

Jesus says to our hearts, *HERE I AM! I STAND AT THE DOOR AND KNOCK. IF ANYONE HEARS MY VOICE AND OPENS THE DOOR, I WILL COME IN.*[5]

Then He says, *TAKE MY YOKE UPON YOU AND LEARN FROM ME, FOR I AM GENTLE AND HUMBLE IN HEART.*[6] And *BLESSED ARE THE MEEK, FOR THEY WILL INHERIT THE EARTH.*[7]

The wisdom that comes from heaven is first of all pure; then peace loving, considerate, submissive.[8] And since *the fruit of the Spirit is. . .gentleness,*[9] we should ask God to develop in us *the unfading beauty of a gentle and quiet spirit, which is of great worth in God's sight.*[10]

[1]2 Corinthians 10:1
[2]Matthew 26:53
[3]Matthew 21:5
[4]Philippians 2:5-8
[5]Revelation 3:20
[6]Matthew 11:29
[7]Matthew 5:5
[8]James 3:17
[9]Galatians 5:22,23
[10]1 Peter 3:4

GOD IS GOOD

He makes others happy by meeting their needs and helping them to live the best life.

The Lord God has *abundant goodness[1]* and *the LORD is good to all.[2]* In fact, when *Moses said, "Now show me your glory," the LORD said, "I will cause all my goodness to pass in front of you."[3]*

This was so important that Jesus said, NO ONE IS GOOD—EXCEPT GOD ALONE.[4]

Every good and perfect gift is from above, coming down from the Father of the heavenly lights.[5] Jesus, God's perfect gift, said, *I AM THE GOOD SHEPHERD. THE GOOD SHEPHERD LAYS DOWN HIS LIFE*

FOR THE SHEEP.[6]

The LORD is good, a refuge in times of trouble.[7] He brings us to Himself through Jesus because *the LORD is good to those whose hope is in him, to the one who seeks him.*[8]

Yes, God's goodness reaches out to us. *Good and upright is the LORD; therefore he instructs sinners in his ways.*[9] He even grows His goodness in us since the *fruit of the Spirit is. . .goodness.*[10]

Taste and see that the LORD is good.[11] And after *you have tasted that the Lord is good,*[12] then *give thanks to the LORD Almighty, for the LORD is good.*[13]

Lord God, *you are good, and what you do is good.*[14] *How great is your goodness, which you have stored up for those who fear you, which you bestow in*

*the sight of men on those who take refuge
in you.*[15]

[1]Psalm 145:7
[2]Psalm 145:9
[3]Exodus 33:18,19
[4]Luke 18:19
[5]James 1:17
[6]John 10:11
[7]Nahum 1:7
[8]Lamentations 3:25
[9]Psalm 25:8
[10]Galatians 5:22
[11]Psalm 34:8
[12]1 Peter 2:3
[13]Jeremiah 33:11
[14]Psalm 119:68
[15]Psalm 31:19

God Is
Gracious

He does good things for people even
though they deserve the opposite.

The Lord your God is gracious.[1] He
is *the God of all grace.*[2] And He calls
Himself *"The Lord, the Lord, the com-
passionate and gracious God."*[3] His
Spirit is *the Spirit of grace.*[4] Indeed, *the
Lord longs to be gracious to you.*[5]

The gospel is God's good news to us
about what Jesus has done for us. It is *the
gospel of God's grace.*[6] *For the grace of
God that brings salvation has appeared
all men.*[7] And *this grace was given
us in Christ Jesus before the beginning
of time.*[8] Actually, *the Law was given
through Moses, grace and truth came
through Jesus Christ.*[9]

It is through the grace of our Lord Jesus that we are saved.[10] God's method was that *while we were still sinners, Christ died for us.*[11] So now we can experience *the incomparable riches of his grace, expressed in his kindness to us in Christ Jesus.*[12]

You know the grace of our Lord Jesus Christ, that though he was rich, yet for your sakes he became poor, so that you through his poverty might become rich.[13]

Through *God's abundant provision of grace*[14] we are *justified freely by his grace.*[15] Then we can say, *by the grace of God I am what I am.*[16]

We should *continue in the grace of God.*[17] And we should *approach the throne of grace with confidence, so that we may receive mercy and find grace to help us in our time of need.*[18]

[1] 2 Chronicles 30:9
[2] 1 Peter 5:10
[3] Exodus 34:6
[4] Hebrews 10:29
[5] Isaiah 30:18
[6] Acts 20:24
[7] Titus 2:11
[8] 2 Timothy 1:9
[9] John 1:17
[10] Acts 15:11
[11] Romans 5:8
[12] Ephesians 2:7
[13] 2 Corinthians 8:9
[14] Romans 5:17
[15] Romans 3:24
[16] 1 Corinthians 15:10
[17] Acts 13:43
[18] Hebrews 4:16

GOD IS HOLY

His perfect goodness and purity set Him apart from all others.

The LORD our God is holy[1] and majestic in holiness.[2] He says, I the LORD am the Holy One.[3]

The ones in heaven proclaim, *Holy, holy, holy is the Lord God Almighty, who was, and is, and is to come.[4] You alone are holy.[5]*

We believe *the holy God will show himself holy by his righteousness.[6]*

God wants us to share in His holiness. This can happen because the same one who says, *Be holy because I, the LORD your God, am holy,[7]* also says, *I am the LORD, who makes you holy.*[8]

How does this holiness come to us? Those who believe in the Lord are part of His church, and *Christ loved the church and gave himself up for her to make her holy.*[9]

So now, *if we walk in the light, as he is in the light, we have fellowship with one another, and the blood of Jesus, his Son, purifies us from all sin.*[10] This way we *put on the new self, created to be like God in true righteousness and holiness.*[11]

Remember, *God disciplines us for our good, that we may share in his holiness.*[12] *This is what the high and lofty One says— he who lives forever, whose name is holy: "I live in a high and holy place, but also with him who is contrite and lowly in spirit, to revive the spirit of the lowly and to revive the heart of the contrite."*[13]

May he strengthen your hearts so that you will be blameless and holy in the presence of our God and Father when our Lord Jesus comes with all his holy ones.[14]

[1]Psalm 99:9
[2]Exodus 15:11
[3]Ezekiel 39:7
[4]Revelation 4:8
[5]Revelation 15:4
[6]Isaiah 5:16
[7]Leviticus 19:2
[8]Leviticus 20:8
[9]Ephesians 5:25,26
[10]1 John 1:7
[11]Ephesians 4:24
[12]Hebrews 12:10
[13]Isaiah 57:15
[14]1 Thessalonians 3:13

GOD IS IMPARTIAL

He looks on the heart and is not swayed by the position, wealth, or appearance of people.

God does not show favoritism.[1] The LORD does not look at the things man looks at. Man looks at the outward appearance, but the LORD looks at the heart.[2]

He shows no partiality to princes and does not favor the rich over the poor, for they are all the work of his hands.[3]

I the LORD search the heart and examine the mind, to reward a man according to his conduct, according to what his deeds deserve.[4]

God does not judge by external ap-pearance.[5] Instead, *the LORD searches every heart and understands every motive behind the thoughts.[6]*

The good news is *that God does not show favoritism but accepts men from every nation who fear him and do what is right.[7]*

So now *you are all sons of God through faith in Christ Jesus. . .there is neither Jew nor Greek, slave nor free, male nor female, for you are all one in Christ Jesus.[8]*

Therefore, *my brothers, as believ-ers in our glorious Lord Jesus Christ, don't show favoritism,[9]* since their *Master and yours is in heaven, and there is no favoritism with him.[10]*

[1]Romans 2:11
[2]1 Samuel 16:7
[3]Job 34:19
[4]Jeremiah 17:10
[5]Galatians 2:6
[6]1 Chronicles 28:9
[7]Acts 10:34,35
[8]Galatians 3:26,28
[9]James 2:1
[10]Ephesians 6:9

GOD IS
JEALOUS

He loves His people so much that He doesn't want them to serve or to be devoted to any other.

I, the LORD your God, am a jealous God.[1] The people were told, *do not worship any other god, for the LORD, whose name is Jealous, is a jealous God.*[2] And again it says, *do not follow other gods, the gods of the peoples around you; for the LORD your God, who is among you, is a jealous God.*[3]

Even though *IT IS WRITTEN: "WORSHIP THE LORD YOUR GOD, AND SERVE HIM ONLY".*[4] *They made him jealous with their foreign gods.*[5] They forgot *he is a holy God; he is a jealous God.*[6] We should not make the same mistake. *Are we trying to* arouse the Lord's jealousy?[7]

If anyone loves the world, the love of the Father is not in him.[8] So, commit yourselves to the LORD and serve him only.[9]

The truth is: *NO SERVANT CAN SERVE TWO MASTERS. EITHER HE WILL HATE THE ONE AND LOVE THE OTHER, OR HE WILL BE DEVOTED TO THE ONE AND DESPISE THE OTHER. YOU CANNOT SERVE BOTH GOD AND MONEY.*[10]

Godly leaders have said: *"I have chosen the way of truth."*[11] And *"I am jealous for you with a godly jealousy."*[12] So choose for yourselves this day whom you will serve. . .But as for me and my household, we will serve the LORD.[13]

I said to the LORD, "You are my Lord; apart from you I have no good thing."[14] I trust in you, O LORD; I say, you

are my God. My times are in your
hands.[15] Whom have I in heaven, but you?
And earth has nothing I desire besides
you.[16]

[1]Exodus 20:5
[2]Exodus 34:14
[3]Deuteronomy 6:14,15
[4]Matthew 4:10
[5]Deuteronomy 32:16
[6]Joshua 24:19
[7]1 Corinthians 10:22
[8]1 John 2:15
[9]1 Samuel 7:3
[10]Luke 16:13
[11]Psalm 119:30
[12]2 Corinthians 11:2
[13]Joshua 24:15
[14]Psalm 16:2
[15]Psalm 31:14,15
[16]Psalm 73:25

GOD IS
JOYFUL

He is never discouraged or depressed but always has a cheerful positive attitude.

The LORD has joy in Himself and in His people. *Your God will rejoice over you.*[1] Yes, *he will rejoice over you with singing.*[2] This joyful attitude gives inward power: *The joy of the LORD is your strength.*[3]

Our example is *Jesus, full of joy through the Holy Spirit.*[4] We see this inward strength in *Jesus, the author and perfecter of our faith, who for the joy set before him endured the cross.*[5] Jesus wants His followers to experience joy. He said, *I HAVE TOLD YOU THIS SO THAT MY JOY MAY BE IN YOU AND THAT YOUR JOY MAY BE COMPLETE.*[6]

As we trust in Him we learn that *the kingdom of God is. . .righteousness, peace and joy in the Holy Spirit.*[7] This is *the joy given by the Holy Spirit.*[8] Because *the fruit of the Spirit is. . .joy.*[9]

Actually, THERE IS REJOICING IN THE PRESENCE OF THE ANGELS OF GOD OVER ONE SINNER WHO REPENTS.[10] And then, *God will rejoice in doing them good.*[11] *Everlasting joy will crown their heads. Gladness and joy will overtake them, and sorrow and sighing will flee away.*[12]

In all our troubles my joy knows no bounds.[13] *May the God of hope fill you with all joy and peace as you trust in him.*[14] *Though you have not seen him, you love him; and even though you do not see him now, you believe in him and are filled with an inexpressible and glorious joy.*[15]

[1]Isaiah 62:5
[2]Zephaniah 3:17
[3]Nehemiah 8:10
[4]Luke 10:21
[5]Hebrews 12:2
[6]John 15:11
[7]Romans 14:17
[8]1 Thessalonians 1:6
[9]Galatians 5:22
[10]Luke 15:10
[11]Jeremiah 32:41
[12]Isaiah 35:10
[13]2 Corinthians 7:4
[14]Romans 15:13
[15]1 Peter 1:8

GOD IS JUST/RIGHTEOUS

He fairly applies His unchanging standards to each situation .

The LORD. . .is righteous; he does no wrong. Morning by morning he dispenses his justice.[1] Indeed, *the LORD works righteousness and justice for all the oppressed.[2]*

In fact, *it is unthinkable that God would do wrong, that the Almighty would pervert justice.[3]* Because *righteousness and justice are the foundation of his throne.[4]*

Truthfully, God's people declare, *Righteous are you, O LORD, and your laws are right.[5] Just and true are your ways, King of the ages.[6]*

In all that has happened to us, you have been just.[7] A faithful God who does no wrong, upright and just is he.[8]

God transfers His righteousness to cover our sins. *This is the name by which he will be called: The LORD Our Righteousness.[9] This righteousness from God comes through faith in Jesus Christ to all who believe.[10] Christ died for sins once for all, the righteous for the unrighteous, to bring you to God.[11]*

How could a just God accept a sinful people? God presented Jesus as the one who would turn aside His wrath, taking away sin, *through faith in his blood* (death for us). . .*he did it to demonstrate his justice. . .so as to be just and the one who justifies the man who has faith in Jesus.[12]*

So, *if we confess our sins, he is faithful*

*and just and will forgive us our sins and
purify us from all unrighteousness.*[13]

[1]Zephaniah 3:5
[2]Psalm 103:6
[3]Job 34:12
[4]Psalm 97:2
[5]Psalm 119:137
[6]Revelation 15:3
[7]Nehemiah 9:33
[8]Deuteronomy 32:4
[9]Jeremiah 23:6
[10]Romans 3:22
[11]1 Peter 3:18
[12]Romans 3:25,26
[13]1 John 1:9

GOD IS KIND

He tenderly reaches down to those who are weak or hurting to make things better.

We say, *You are kind and forgiving, O LORD, abounding in love to all who call to you.*[1] He says, *I am the LORD, who exercises kindness. . .on earth.*[2]

About His people He said, *I led them with cords of human kindness.*[3] Then His people can *tell of the kindness of the LORD, the deeds for which he is to be praised.*[4]

THE MOST HIGH. . .IS KIND TO THE UN-GRATEFUL AND WICKED.[5] People should appreciate *the riches of his kindness. . . realizing that God's kindness leads you toward repentance.*[6]

God's kindness opens the door for us to come to Him. Because *love is kind,[7] when the kindness and love of God our Savior appeared, he saved us.[8]*

And then, *in the coming ages he might show the incomparable riches of his grace, expressed in his kindness to us in Christ Jesus.[9]*

God puts His kindness into us, since *the fruit of the Spirit is. . .kindness.[10]* Then we can *be kind and compassionate to one another, forgiving each other, just as in Christ God forgave you.[11]*

Consider therefore the kindness and sternness of God: sternness to those who fell, but kindness to you, provided that you continue in his kindness.[12]

[1]Psalm 86:5
[2]Jeremiah 9:24
[3]Hosea 11:4
[4]Isaiah 63:7
[5]Luke 6:35
[6]Romans 2:4
[7]1 Corinthians 13:4
[8]Titus 3:4,5
[9]Ephesians 2:7
[10]Galatians 5:22
[11]Ephesians 4:32
[12]Romans 11:22

GOD IS LOVING

He happily gives of Himself so that He can share life with others.

The LORD is. . .loving toward all he has made.[1] He is abounding in love.[2] As high as the heavens are above the earth, so great is his love for those who fear him.[3] From everlasting to everlasting the LORD's love is with those who fear him.[4]

God demonstrates his own love for us in this: While we were still sinners, Christ died for us.[5] Yes, this is how God showed his love among us: he sent his one and only Son into the world that we might live through him.[6]

I pray that you. . .may have power . . .to grasp how wide and long and high and deep is the love of Christ, and to know this love that surpasses knowledge.[7]

We know and rely on the love God has for us.[8] And we love because he first loved us.[9] So now, though you have not seen him, you love him.[10]

When you live with God you discover that you yourselves have been taught by God to love each other.[11] This takes place because God has poured out his love into our hearts by the Holy Spirit, whom he has given us.[12] When the Spirit of God cultivates our lives we see that the fruit of the Spirit is love.[13]

Yes, may the Lord direct your hearts into God's love.[14] Remember that neither death nor life, neither angels nor demons, neither the present nor the future, nor any powers, neither height nor depth, nor

*anything else in all creation, will be able
to separate us from the love of God that is
in Christ Jesus our Lord.*[15]

[1]Psalm 145:13
[2]Psalm 103:8
[3]Psalm 103:11
[4]Psalm 103:17
[5]Romans 5:8
[6]1 John 4:9
[7]Ephesians 3:17-19
[8]1 John 4:16
[9]1 John 4:19
[10]1 Peter 1:8
[11]1 Thessalonians 4:9
[12]Romans 5:5
[13]Galatians 5:22
[14]2 Thessalonians 3:5
[15]Romans 8:38,39

GOD IS PATIENT

He is not in a rush and can be at peace with the slow progress of people.

We believe in *the LORD, the LORD, the compassionate and gracious God, slow to anger.*[1] Isaiah talked of *"the patience of my God."*[2] And Paul referred to *the riches of his kindness, tolerance and patience.*[3]

In early times *God waited patiently in the days of Noah while the ark was being built.*[4] Later, a leader of God's people recognized, *For many years you were patient with them. By your Spirit you admonished them through your prophets.*[5]

Paul said, *I was shown mercy so that in me, the worst of sinners, Christ Jesus might display his unlimited patience as an example for those who would believe on him and receive eternal life.*[6]

You see, *he is patient with you, not wanting anyone to perish, but everyone to come to repentance.*[7] This is because *our Lord's patience means salvation.*[8]

Not only is God patient with us, but He also teaches us to be patient. *The fruit of the Spirit is. . .patience.*[9] When we really have His love we find that *love is patient.*[10]

If we come to know *the God who gives endurance and encouragement,*[11] then we can have the *patient endurance that is ours in Jesus.*[12]

[1]Exodus 34:6
[2]Isaiah 7:13
[3]Romans 2:4
[4]1 Peter 3:20
[5]Nehemiah 9:30
[6]1 Timothy 1:16
[7]2 Peter 3:9
[8]2 Peter 3:15
[9]Galatians 5:22
[10]1 Corinthians 13:4
[11]Romans 15:5
[12]Revelation 1:9

GOD IS PEACEFUL

He is not disturbed, upset, or worried by any circumstances.

We believe in the One called *the God of peace.¹* Peace is more than just the absence of outward conflicts. It is that amazing inner calm called *the peace of God, which transcends all understanding.²*

This was shown in the life of Jesus. Once, *as they sailed, he fell asleep. A squall came down on the lake, so that the boat was being swamped, and they were in great danger. The disciples went and woke him, saying, "Master, Master, we're going to drown!" he got up and rebuked the wind and the raging waters; the storm subsided, and all was calm.³*

This is what His followers later called *the peace of Christ.*[4] To His followers, Jesus said, *PEACE I LEAVE WITH YOU; MY PEACE I GIVE TO YOU. . .DO NOT LET YOUR HEARTS BE TROUBLED AND DO NOT BE AFRAID.*[5]

The Lord promised, *My presence will go with you, and I will give you rest.*[6] And Jesus repeated this by saying, *TAKE MY YOKE UPON YOU AND LEARN FROM ME, FOR I AM GENTLE AND HUMBLE IN HEART, AND YOU WILL FIND REST FOR YOUR SOULS.*[7]

The LORD gives strength to his people; the LORD blesses his people with peace.[8] In fact, *the kingdom of God is. . . righteousness, peace and joy in the Holy Spirit.*[9] When we direct our thoughts and values toward God, we discover that *the mind controlled by the Spirit is life and peace.*[10] Yes, *the fruit of the Spirit is. . . peace.*[11]

*May the Lord of peace himself give
you peace at all times and in every way.[12]*

[1]Romans 15:33
[2]Philippians 4:7
[3]Luke 8:23-24
[4]Colossians 3:15
[5]John 14:27
[6]Exodus 33:14
[7]Matthew 11:29
[8]Psalm 29:11
[9]Romans 14:17
[10]Romans 8:6
[11]Galatians 5:22
[12]2 Thessalonians 3:16

God Is Seeking

He does not wait for people to find Him; instead, He reaches out to people so they can know Him.

God looks for people open to Him. *The eyes of the LORD range throughout the earth to strengthen those whose hearts are fully committed to him.*[1] He did not hide Himself. *He made known his ways to Moses, his deeds to the people of Israel.*[2]

He wants us to come to Him: *As surely as I live, declares the Sovereign LORD, I take no pleasure in the death of the wicked, but rather that they turn from their ways and live.*[3] Then *THE TRUE WORSHIPERS WILL WORSHIP THE FATHER IN SPIRIT AND TRUTH, FOR THEY ARE THE KIND*

OF WORSHIPERS THE FATHER SEEKS.[4]

Jesus, *THE SON OF MAN, CAME TO SEEK AND TO SAVE WHAT WAS LOST.*[5] He said, *I DID NOT COME TO JUDGE THE WORLD, BUT TO SAVE IT.*[6] *I HAVE COME THAT THEY MIGHT HAVE LIFE, AND HAVE IT TO THE FULL.*[7]

Once, *on the last and greatest day of the Feast, Jesus stood and said in a loud voice, "IF A MAN IS THIRSTY, LET HIM COME TO ME AND DRINK."*[8] He says to our hearts, *HERE I AM! I STAND AT THE DOOR AND KNOCK. IF ANYONE HEARS MY VOICE AND OPENS THE DOOR, I WILL COME IN.*[9]

COME TO ME, ALL YOU WHO ARE WEARY AND BURDENED, AND I WILL GIVE YOU REST. TAKE MY YOKE UPON YOU AND LEARN FROM ME, FOR I AM GENTLE AND HUMBLE IN HEART, AND YOU WILL FIND REST FOR YOUR SOULS.[10]

We are therefore Christ's ambassadors, as though God were making his appeal through us. We implore you on Christ's behalf: Be reconciled to God.[11] Our message is, *Whoever is thirsty, let him come; and whoever wishes, let him take the free gift of the water of life.[12]*

[1]2 Chronicles 16:9
[2]Psalm 103:7
[3]Ezekiel 33:11
[4]John 4:23
[5]Luke 19:10
[6]John 12:47
[7]John 10:10
[8]John 7:37
[9]Revelation 3:20
[10]Matthew 11:28,29
[11]2 Corinthians 5:20
[12]Revelation 22:17

GOD IS TRUTHFUL

All of His statements are reliable and He never contradicts Himself.

We put our trust in *the God of truth.*[1] He is the *God who does not lie,*[2] because *it is impossible for God to lie.*[3] Therefore, *the word of the LORD is right and true.*[4] And we can declare, *your words are trustworthy.*[5]

We believe in Jesus, *the one and only Son, who came from the Father, full of grace and truth.*[6] In fact, *grace and truth came through Jesus Christ.*[7]

He said, FOR THIS I CAME INTO THE WORLD, TO TESTIFY TO THE TRUTH. EVERYONE ON THE SIDE OF TRUTH LISTENS TO ME.[8] And, *I AM THE WAY AND THE TRUTH*

AND THE LIFE. NO ONE COMES TO THE FATHER EXCEPT THROUGH ME.[9]

John wrote that his book about Jesus was *written that you may believe that Jesus is the Christ, the Son of God, and that by believing you may have life in his name.*[10]

We accept *the word of truth, the gospel.*[11] You see, *God our Savior wants all men to be saved and to come to a knowledge of the truth.*[12] And *he chose to give us birth through the word of truth.*[13] So that we are *saved . . .through belief in the truth.*[14]

Jesus said, *GOD IS SPIRIT, AND HIS WORSHIPERS MUST WORSHIP IN SPIRIT AND IN TRUTH.*[15] For *YOU WILL KNOW THE TRUTH, AND THE TRUTH WILL SET YOU FREE.*[16]

Now we can say to God, *your word*

is a lamp to my feet and a light for my path.[17] And may your love and your truth always protect me.[18]

[1]Isaiah 65:16
[2]Titus 1:2
[3]Hebrews 6:18
[4]Psalm 33:4
[5]2 Samuel 7:28
[6]John 1:14
[7]John 1:17
[8]John 18:37
[9]John 14:6
[10]John 20:31
[11]Ephesians 1:13
[12]1 Timothy 2:3,4
[13]James 1:18
[14]2 Thessalonians 2:13
[15]John 4:24
[16]John 8:32
[17]Psalm 119:105
[18]Psalm 40:11

God Is Wise

He knows the right thing to do at all times and in all situations.

To God belong wisdom and power; counsel and understanding are his.[1] He is *the only wise God.*[2] We look at nature and realize that *by wisdom the Lord laid the earth's foundations.*[3]

Oh, the depth of the riches of the wisdom and knowledge of God![4] Yes, *his understanding has no limit.*[5]

But, *there is a God in heaven who reveals mysteries.*[6] We can *know the mystery of God, namely, Christ, in whom are hidden all the treasures of wisdom and knowledge.*[7]

Actually, Jesus Christ was filled with *the Spirit of the LORD. . .the Spirit of wisdom and understanding.*[8] Now to some He is offensive or foolish, but to us who believe, *Jesus is Christ the power of God and the wisdom of God.*[9]

We are not on our own. The LORD *gives wisdom.*[10] Jesus said, *I WILL GIVE YOU WORDS AND WISDOM THAT NONE OF YOUR ADVERSARIES WILL BE ABLE TO RESIST OR CONTRADICT.*[11]

You see, *his intent was that now, through the church, the manifold wisdom of God should be made known.*[12]

Remember, *if any of you lacks wisdom, he should ask God, who gives generously to all without finding fault, and it will be given to him.*[11]

We can say to God, *"you teach me*

wisdom in the inmost place."[14]

[1]Job 12:13
[2]Romans 16:27
[3]Proverbs 3:19
[4]Romans 11:33
[5]Psalm 147:5
[6]Daniel 2:28
[7]Colossians 2:2,3
[8]Isaiah 11:2
[9]1 Corinthians 1:24
[10]Proverbs 2:6
[11]Luke 21:15
[12]Ephesians 3:10
[13]James 1:5
[14]Psalm 51:6

GOD IS WRATHFUL

He is greatly displeased by the wrongs that people do; because they hurt others, they hurt themselves, and they insult His authority.

The LORD is the true God; he is the living God, the eternal King. When he is angry the earth trembles; the nations cannot endure his wrath.[1] God is a righteous judge, a God who expresses his wrath every day.[2]

In specific, *God's wrath comes on those who are disobedient.[3]* Yes, *the wrath of God is being revealed from heaven against all the godlessness and wickedness of men who suppress the truth by their wickedness.[4]* In other words, *for those who are self-seeking and* who reject the truth and follow evil, there will be wrath and anger.[5]

When Jesus encountered people who opposed the truth, even He *looked around at them in anger. . .deeply distressed at their stubborn hearts.*[6]

The two choices we have are: *whoever believes in the Son has eternal life, but whoever rejects the Son will not see life, for God's wrath remains on him.*[7]

In fact, *God did not appoint us to suffer wrath but to receive salvation through our Lord Jesus Christ.*[8] This way we shall *be saved from God's wrath through him.*[9]

Jesus, who rescues us from the coming wrath[10] said, GOD DID NOT SEND HIS SON INTO THE WORLD TO CONDEMN THE WORLD, BUT TO SAVE THE WORLD THROUGH HIM.[11]

Like the rest, we were by nature objects of wrath. But because of his great love for us, God, who is rich in mercy, made us alive with Christ even when we were dead in transgressions.[12]

[1]Jeremiah 10:10
[2]Psalm 7:11
[3]Ephesians 5:6
[4]Romans 1:18
[5]Romans 2:8
[6]Mark 3:5
[7]John 3:36
[8]1 Thessalonians 5:9
[9]Romans 5:9
[10]1 Thessalonians 1:10
[11]John 3:17
[12]Ephesians 2:3-5

NOTES

_____

_____

_____

_____

_____

_____

_____

_____

_____

_____

_____

_____

_____

_____

_____

_____

NOTES

THE
ROLES
OF
GOD

GOD IS
OUR COMFORTER

He soothes the internal hurts that are part of this life.

The LORD comforts his people.[1] God, who comforts the downcast [2] is the Father of compassion and God of all comfort.[3]

BLESSED ARE THOSE WHO MOURN, FOR THEY SHALL BE COMFORTED.[4] One day God will wipe away every tear from their eyes.[5]

God says, *I, even I, am he who comforts you.[6] As a mother comforts her child, so I will comfort you.[7]*

I am the LORD, your God, who takes hold of your right hand and says to you, Do not fear; I will help you.[8] I will guide him and restore comfort to him.[9]

Indeed, Jesus said, *I HAVE TOLD YOU THESE THINGS, SO THAT IN ME YOU MAY HAVE PEACE. IN THIS WORLD YOU WILL HAVE TROUBLE. BUT TAKE HEART! I HAVE OVERCOME THE WORLD.*[10]

God comforts us through *THE COUNSELOR, THE HOLY SPIRIT*[11] and through *the encouragement of the Scriptures.*[12]

By faith, we can pray, *may your unfailing love be my comfort, according to your promise.*[13] Then we can state, *you, O LORD, have helped me and comforted me.*[14] *My comfort in my suffering is this: your promise renews my life.*[15]

Praise be to the God and Father of our Lord Jesus Christ, the Father of compassion and God of all comfort, who comforts us in all our troubles, so

*that we can comfort those in any trou-
ble with the comfort we ourselves have
received from God.*[16]

[1]Isaiah 49:13
[2]2 Corinthians 7:6
[3]2 Corinthians 1:3
[4]Matthew 5:4
[5]Revelation 7:17
[6]Isaiah 51:12
[7]Isaiah 66:13
[8]Isaiah 41:13
[9]Isaiah 57:18
[10]John 16:33
[11]John 14:26
[12]Romans 15:4
[13]Psalm 119:76
[14]Psalm 86:17
[15]Psalm 119:50
[16]2 Corinthians 1:3,4

God Is
The Creator

The physical universe was made by Him
and He continues to keep it in existence.

*The LORD is the everlasting God,
the Creator of the ends of the earth.*[1] In
*space. . .he suspends the earth over
nothing.*[2] Yes, *the LORD made the heavens and the earth, the sea, and all that
is in them.*[3]

He said, *It is I who made the earth
and created mankind upon it. My own
hands stretched out the heavens; I marshaled their starry hosts.*[4] So, *by faith we
understand that the universe was formed
at God's command.*[5]

*In these last days he has spoken to us
by his Son, whom he appointed heir of all*

things, and through whom he made the universe.[6] Indeed, by *him all things were created: things in heaven and on earth, visible and invisible. . .he is before all things, and in him all things hold together.*[7] *In his hand is the life of every creature and the breath of all mankind.*[8]

He promised, I will create new heavens and a new earth.[9] When this happens *the creation itself will be liberated from its bondage to decay and brought into the glorious freedom of the children of God.*[10] Yes, *we are looking forward to a new heaven and a new earth, the home of righteousness.*[11]

God's creative work is seen in our lives. *We are God's workmanship, created in Christ Jesus to do good works, which God prepared in advance for us to do.*[12] This happens because *if anyone is in Christ, he is a new creation; the old has gone, the new has come!* [13]

If we can say: *The Spirit of God has made me; the breath of the Almighty gives me life,* [14] then we should pray: *Create in me a pure heart, O God, and renew a steadfast spirit within me.* [15]

[1]Isaiah 40:28
[2]Job 26:7
[3]Exodus 20:11
[4]Isaiah 45:12
[5]Hebrews 11:3
[6]Hebrews 1:2
[7]Colossians 1:16,17
[8]Job 12:10
[9]Isaiah 65:17
[10]Romans 8:21
[11]2 Peter 3:13
[12]Ephesians 2:10
[13]2 Corinthians 5:17
[14]Job 33:4
[15]Psalm 51:10

GOD IS
OUR FATHER

He raises His children through proper care, direction, and instruction so they can mature.

We believe in *one God and Father of all, who is over all and through all and in all.[1] For us there is but one God, the Father, from whom all things came and for whom we live.[2]* He is not only *the God of our Lord Jesus Christ, the glorious Father,[3]* but also *a father to the fatherless . . .is God.[4]*

"I will be a Father to you, and you will be my sons and daughters," says the Lord Almighty.[5]

How great is the love the Father has lavished on us, that we should be called

*children of God!⁶ And now, because you
are sons, God sent the Spirit of his Son
into our hearts, the Spirit who calls out,
"Abba, Father."⁷*

*O LORD, you are our Father. We are
the clay, you are the potter; we are all
the work of your hand.⁸*

The Father provided Jesus. He said,
IT IS MY FATHER WHO GIVES YOU THE TRUE
BREAD FROM HEAVEN. . .I AM THE BREAD OF
LIFE. . .EVERYONE WHO LISTENS TO THE
FATHER AND LEARNS FROM HIM COMES TO
ME. . .JUST AS THE LIVING FATHER SENT ME
AND I LIVE BECAUSE OF THE FATHER, SO THE
ONE WHO FEEDS ON ME WILL LIVE BECAUSE
OF ME.⁹

You may have a flawed earthly
father, but with God you can *call on a
Father who judges each man's work
impartially.¹⁰* How much more should we

submit to the Father of our spirits and live! Our fathers disciplined us for a little while as they thought best; but God disciplines us for our good, that we may share in his holiness. . .It produces a harvest of righteousness and peace for those who have been trained by it.[11]

[1]Ephesians 4:6
[2]1 Corinthians 8:6
[3]Ephesians 1:17
[4]Psalm 68:5
[5]2 Corinthians 6:18
[6]1 John 3:1
[7]Galatians 4:6
[8]Isaiah 64:8
[9]John 6:32,35,45,57
[10]1 Peter 1:17
[11]Hebrews 12:9-11

God Is
Our Guide

He helps His people to take the best paths for their lives.

This God is our God for ever and ever; he will be our guide even to the end.[1] *he guides the humble in what is right and teaches them his way.*[2] Indeed, *he who has compassion on them will guide them.*[3]

If you can say, *"he leads me,"*[4] then realize that *those who are led by the Spirit of God are sons of God.*[5] And *remember how the LORD your God led you all the way. . .to humble you and to test you in order to know what was in your heart, whether or not you would keep his commands.*[6]

To seekers, God says, *I will lead the*

blind by ways they have not known, along unfamiliar paths I will guide them; I will turn the darkness into light before them and make the rough places smooth. These are the things I will do; I will not forsake them.[7]

In the past, *I led them with cords of human kindness, with ties of love.*[8] And now, *whether you turn to the right or to the left, your ears will hear a voice behind you, saying, "This is the way; walk in it."*[9]

Say to God, *you guide me with your counsel, and afterward you will take me into glory.*[10] Even *if I settle on the far side of the sea, even there your hand will guide me, your right hand will hold me fast.*[11]

Yes, *lead me, O LORD, in your righteousness. . . make straight your way before me.*[12] *Show me your ways, O*

Lord, teach me your paths; guide me in your truth and teach me, for you are God my Savior, and my hope is in you all day long.[13] May your good Spirit lead me on level ground.[14]

[1]Psalm 48:14
[2]Psalm 25:9
[3]Isaiah 49:10
[4]Psalm 23:2
[5]Romans 8:14
[6]Deuteronomy 8:2
[7]Isaiah 42:16
[8]Hosea 11:4
[9]Isaiah 30:21
[10]Psalm 73:24
[11]Psalm 139:9,10
[12]Psalm 5:8
[13]Psalm 25:4,5
[14]Psalm 143:10

GOD IS THE HEALER

He restores physical, emotional, and spiritual well-being according to His loving plan.

"I will restore you to health and heal your wounds" declares the LORD.[1] God deals with our inner problems and our outer problems: *He forgives all my sins and heals all my diseases.*[2]

When our emotions are hurt *he heals the brokenhearted and binds up their wounds.*[3] As we learn sympathy for others we discover that *blessed is the man who has regard for the weak. . .the LORD will sustain him on his sickbed and restore him from his bed of illness.*[4]

Jesus demonstrated the healing work

of God. Once, *when evening came, many who were demon-possessed were brought to him, and he drove out the spirits with a word and healed all the sick. This was to fulfill what was spoken through the prophet Isaiah: "he took up our infirmities and carried our diseases."*[5]

Yes, Jesus provided for our spiritual healing since *he himself bore our sins in his body on the* (cross), *so that we might die to sins and live for righteousness; by his wounds you have been healed.*[6]

Peter, a follower of Jesus, had to ask the crowd of onlookers, *Why do you stare at us as if by our own power or godliness we had made this* (crippled) *man walk?. . .It is Jesus' name and the faith that comes through him that has given this complete healing to him.*[7]

With these things in mind, we can

pray, *O LORD, have mercy on me; heal me, for I have sinned against you.*[8] *Be merciful to me, LORD, for I am faint; O LORD, heal me, for my bones are in agony.*[9] *heal me, O LORD, and I will be healed; save me and I will be saved.*[10]

[1]Jeremiah 30:17
[2]Psalm 103:3
[3]Psalm 147:3
[4]Psalm 41:1,3
[5]Matthew 8:16,17
[6]1 Peter 2:24
[7]Acts 3:12,16
[8]Psalm 41:4
[9]Psalm 6:2
[10]Jeremiah 17:14

GOD IS
THE JUDGE

He fairly and correctly decides if each person has done what He wanted them to do.

Surely there is a God who judges the earth.[1] He is the LORD, the Judge.[2] He is God, the judge of all men.[3]

There is only one Lawgiver and Judge.[4] And each person will have to give account to him who is ready to judge the living and the dead.[5]

God is a righteous judge.[6] he will judge the world in righteousness and the peoples in his truth.[7]

Now *all a man's ways seem innocent to him, but motives are weighed by the*

LORD.*[8]* Indeed, *God will judge men's secrets through Jesus Christ.*[9]

He will bring to light what is hidden in darkness and will expose the motives of men's hearts.[10]

I the LORD search the heart and examine the mind.[11]

Christ Jesus, who will judge the living and the dead,[12] said, THE FATHER JUDGES NO ONE, BUT HAS ENTRUSTED ALL JUDGMENT TO THE SON. . .WHOEVER HEARS MY WORD AND BELIEVES HIM WHO SENT ME HAS ETERNAL LIFE AND WILL NOT BE CONDEMNED; HE HAS CROSSED OVER FROM DEATH TO LIFE.[13]

If you, O LORD, kept a record of sins, O LORD, who could stand? But with you there is forgiveness.[14]

Now there is in store for me the crown of righteousness, which the Lord, the righteous Judge, will award to me on that day—and not only to me, but also to all who have longed for his appearing.[15]

[1]Psalm 58:11
[2]Judges 11:27
[3]Hebrews 12:23
[4]James 4:12
[5]1 Peter 4:5
[6]Psalm 7:11
[7]Psalm 96:13
[8]Proverbs 16:2
[9]Romans 2:16
[10]1 Corinthians 4:5
[11]Jeremiah 17:10
[12]2 Timothy 4:1
[13]John 5:22,24
[14]Psalm 130:3,4
[15]2 Timothy 4:8

GOD IS THE KING OF HEAVEN

In the spiritual kingdom of light, He is the revered and unquestioned ruler of all.

The LORD is enthroned as King forever.[1] he does as he pleases with the powers of heaven.[2] How awesome is the LORD Most High, the great King over all the earth![3] The LORD says: "heaven is my throne and the earth is my footstool."[4]

A good prayer would be: *O God, God of the spirits of all mankind.[5] you give life to everything, and the multitudes of heaven worship you.[6] HALLOWED BE YOUR NAME, YOUR KINGDOM COME, YOUR WILL BE DONE ON EARTH AS IT IS IN HEAVEN.[7]*

This applies to Jesus who said, *I CAN*

CALL ON MY FATHER, AND HE WILL AT ONCE PUT AT MY DISPOSAL MORE THAN TWELVE LEGIONS (72,000) *OF ANGELS.*[8] Yes, *WHEN THE SON OF MAN COMES IN HIS GLORY, AND ALL THE ANGELS WITH HIM, HE WILL SIT ON HIS THRONE IN HEAVENLY GLORY.*[9]

When John had heaven revealed to him he *looked and heard the voice of many angels. . .ten thousand times ten thousand. . .In a loud voice they sang: "Worthy is the Lamb* (Jesus), *who was slain, to receive power and wealth and wisdom and strength and honor and glory and praise!"*[10]

How wonderful that *he will command his angels concerning you to guard you in all your ways.*[11] Because *all angels* (are) *ministering spirits sent to serve those who will inherit salvation.*[12]

God said to His people, *See, I am*

*sending an angel ahead of you to guard
you along the way and to bring you to
the place I have prepared.[13]* Now we can
declare, *the Lord will rescue me from
every evil attack and will bring me safely to his heavenly kingdom.[14]*

[1]Psalm 29:10
[2]Daniel 4:35
[3]Psalm 47:2
[4]Isaiah 66:1
[5]Numbers 16:22
[6]Nehemiah 9:6
[7]Matthew 6:9,10
[8]Matthew 26:53
[9]Matthew 25:31
[10]Revelation 5:11,12
[11]Psalm 91:11
[12]Hebrews 1:14
[13]Exodus 23:20
[14]2 Timothy 4:18

GOD IS THE LORD
AND THE LAWGIVER

He tells everyone what to do (law); and
He personally directs His people.

*The LORD is the true God; he is the
living God, the eternal King.[1] There is
only one Lawgiver and Judge;[2] the
Lord is our Lawgiver.[3]*

God says, *Listen to me, my people;
hear me, my nation: The law will go out
from me; my justice will become a light
to the nations.[4] Yes, the law is holy, and
the commandment is holy, righteous and
good.[5]*

But to those who are hypocrites He
says, "WHY DO YOU CALL ME, 'Lord,
Lord', AND DO NOT DO WHAT I SAY?"[6]

The law of the LORD *is perfect, reviving the soul. The statutes of the* LORD *are trustworthy, making wise the simple. The precepts of the* LORD *are right, giving joy to the heart. The commands of the* LORD *are radiant, giving light to the eyes.*[7]

God uses His law to reach us. *The law is good if a man uses it properly. We also know that law is made not for good men but for lawbreakers and rebels, the ungodly and sinful, the unholy and irreligious.*[8] Because *through the law we become conscious of sin.*[9]

We see that *the law was put in charge to lead us to Christ that we might be justified by faith*[10] in Jesus.

In God's plan *the law was given through Moses; grace and truth came through Jesus Christ.*[11] *For what the law was powerless to do in that it was weakened by the sinful nature, God did by sending his own Son in the likeness of sinful man to be a sin offering. . .in order that the righteous requirements of the law might be fully met in us, who do not live according to the sinful nature but according to the Spirit.*[12]

[1]Jeremiah 10:10
[2]James 4:12
[3]Isaiah 33:22
[4]Isaiah 51:4
[5]Romans 7:12
[6]Luke 6:46
[7]Psalm 19:7,8
[8]1 Timothy 1:8,9
[9]Romans 3:20
[10]Galatians 3:24
[11]John 1:17
[12]Romans 8:3,4

GOD IS
OUR PROTECTOR

He guards His people from those physical harms or spiritual attacks which do not serve His purpose.

He guards the course of the just and protects the way of his faithful ones.[1] They through faith are shielded by God's power.[2]

The angel of the LORD encamps around those who fear him, and he delivers them.[3] Yes, Lord, in the shelter of your presence you hide them from the intrigues of men.[4]

I will say of the LORD, "he is my refuge and my fortress, my God, in whom I trust."[5] I know whom I have believed, and am convinced that he is able to guard what I have entrusted to him for that day.[6]

In the day of trouble he will keep me safe.[7] The Lord will rescue me from every evil attack and will bring me safely to his heavenly kingdom. To him be glory for ever and ever.[8]

When an enemy attacks, remember that *with him is only the arm of flesh, but with us is the LORD our God to help us and to fight our battles.[9]*

Trust in *him who is able to keep you from falling and to present you before his glorious presence without fault and with great joy.[10]* Because *his faithfulness will be your shield.[11]* Yes, *the LORD will fight for you; you need only to be still.[12]*

In other words, *do not be anxious about anything, but in everything, by prayer and petition, with thanksgiving,*

*present your requests to God. And the
peace of God, which transcends all
understanding, will guard your hearts
and your minds in Christ Jesus.*[13]

[1]Proverb 2:8
[2]1 Peter 1:5
[3]Psalm 34:7
[4]Psalm 31:20
[5]Psalm 91:2
[6]2 Timothy 1:12
[7]Psalm 27:5
[8]2 Timothy 4:18
[9]2 Chronicles 32:8
[10]Jude 24
[11]Psalm 91:4
[12]Exodus 14:14
[13]Philippians 4:6,7

God Is
Our Provider

He sees to it that the physical, emotional, and spiritual needs of His people are met the best way.

God, *the eyes of all look to you, and you give them their food at the proper time.*[1] Yes, *he provides food for those who fear him.*[2] In His own ways, *the blessing of the LORD brings wealth, and he adds no trouble to it,*[3] unlike the wealth people often obtain.

Truly, *my God will meet all your needs according to his glorious riches in Christ Jesus.*[4] And *those who seek the LORD lack no good thing.*[5]

God takes care of our inner needs also. He looked at Adam, alone in Eden, and *the LORD God said, "It is not good for the man to be alone. I will make a helper suitable for him."⁶*

When His people were oppressed, He *lifted the yoke from their neck and bent down to feed them.⁷*

Do not fear, for I am with you; do not be dismayed, for I am your God. I will strengthen you and help you.⁸ Even to your old age and gray hairs I am he, I am he who will sustain you. I have made you and I will carry you; I will sustain you and I will rescue you.⁹

Jesus said, *DO NOT WORRY, SAYING, "WHAT SHALL WE EAT?" OR "WHAT SHALL WE DRINK?" OR "WHAT SHALL WE WEAR?" FOR THE PAGANS RUN AFTER ALL THESE THINGS, AND YOUR HEAVENLY FATHER KNOWS THAT YOU NEED THEM. BUT SEEK FIRST HIS KINGDOM AND HIS RIGHTEOUSNESS, AND ALL*

THESE THINGS WILL BE GIVEN TO YOU AS WELL.[10]

ASK AND IT WILL BE GIVEN TO YOU; SEEK AND YOU WILL FIND; KNOCK AND THE DOOR WILL BE OPENED TO YOU.[11] *IF YOU. . .KNOW HOW TO GIVE GOOD GIFTS TO YOUR CHILDREN, HOW MUCH MORE WILL YOUR FATHER IN HEAVEN GIVE GOOD GIFTS TO THOSE WHO ASK HIM!*[12]

[1]Psalm 145:15
[2]Psalm 111:5
[3]Proverbs 10:22
[4]Philippians 4:19
[5]Psalm 34:10
[6]Genesis 2:18
[7]Hosea 11:4
[8]Isaiah 41:10
[9]Isaiah 46:4
[10]Matthew 6:31-33
[11]Matthew 7:7
[12]Matthew 7:11

GOD IS THE
RULER OF NATURE

The physical realm apart from mankind is subject to His direction at any time and in any way He chooses.

The LORD is God in heaven above and on the earth below.[1] The LORD does whatever pleases him, in the heavens and on the earth, in the seas and all their depths. He makes clouds rise from the ends of the earth; he sends lightning with the rain and brings out the wind from his storehouses.[2]

He changes times and seasons.[3] He is the LORD our God, who gives autumn and spring rains in season.[4] But, in grace, HE CAUSES HIS SUN TO RISE ON THE EVIL AND THE GOOD, AND SENDS RAIN ON THE RIGHTEOUS AND THE UNRIGHTEOUS.[5]

It is said of God, *you rule over the surging sea; when its waves mount up, you still them.⁶* Jesus showed this during a storm when *he got up and rebuked the wind and the raging waters; the storm subsided, and all was calm.⁷*

Moreover, when Jesus encountered the funeral of an only son *he said, "YOUNG MAN, I SAY TO YOU, GET UP!" The dead man sat up and began to talk, and Jesus gave him back to his mother.⁸*

And when a friend of His died, He went to the tomb and *Jesus called in a loud voice, "LAZARUS, COME OUT!" The dead man came out.⁹*

Some believers who were threatened with harm said, *"If we are thrown into the blazing furnace, the God we serve is able to save us from it, and he will rescue us."¹⁰* Indeed, when they came out *the fire had not harmed their bodies. . . and there was no smell of fire on them.*[11] *This is because the angel of the LORD encamps around those who fear him, and he delivers them.*[12]

[1]Deuteronomy 4:39
[2]Psalm 135:6,7
[3]Daniel 2:21
[4]Jeremiah 5:24
[5]Matthew 5:45
[6]Psalm 89:9
[7]Luke 8:24
[8]Luke 7:14,15
[9]John 11:43,44
[10]Daniel 3:17
[11]Daniel 3:27
[12]Psalm 34:7

God Is The Ruler Over Mankind

Although he chooses not to control anyone's spirit, He has the option of arranging circumstances to His ends.

God reigns over the nations.[1] In other words, He does *guide the nations of the earth.*[2] To Him *all the peoples of the earth are regarded as nothing. He does as he pleases with the powers of heaven and the peoples of the earth.*[3]

As he sees fit *the LORD sends poverty and wealth; he humbles and he exalts.*[4] *he makes nations great, and destroys them; he enlarges nations, and disperses them.*[5]

Man is free to think, and *many are the plans in a man's heart, but it is the LORD's purpose that prevails.*[6] Yes, *in his heart a man plans his course, but the* LORD *determines his steps.*[7] *If a man's steps are directed by the* LORD, *how then can anyone understand his own way?*[8]

He himself gives all men life and breath and everything else. . .he determined the times set for them and the exact places where they should live.[9]

Because *you do not even know what will happen tomorrow. . .you ought to say, "If it is the Lord's will, we will live and do this or that."*[10] And *the* LORD *is with me; I will not be afraid. What can man do to me?*[11]

Lord, *wealth and honor come from you; you are the ruler of all things.*[12]

God says, *I, even I, am he who comforts you. Who are you that you fear mortal men, the sons of men, who are* *but grass, that you forget the L*ORD *your Maker, who stretched out the heavens and laid the foundations of the earth?*[13]

[1]Psalm 47:8
[2]Psalm 67:4
[3]Daniel 4:35
[4]1 Samuel 2:7
[5]Job 12:23
[6]Proverbs 19:21
[7]Proverbs 16:9
[8]Proverbs 20:24
[9]Acts 17:25,26
[10]James 4:14,15
[11]Psalm 118:6
[12]1 Chronicles 29:12
[13]Isaiah 51:12,13

GOD IS OUR SHEPHERD

He feeds, protects, and leads His flock of followers.

He is our God, and we are the people of his pasture, the flock under his care.[1] In fact, *he tends his flock like a shepherd: he gathers the lambs in his arms and carries them close to his heart; he gently leads those that have young.*[2]

We can believe that *the LORD is my shepherd, I shall lack nothing. He makes me lie down in green pastures, he leads me beside quiet waters, he restores my soul.*[3]

You my sheep, the sheep of my pasture, are people, and I am your God,

declares the Sovereign LORD.[4] I myself
will tend my sheep and have them lie
down, declares the Sovereign LORD. I
will search for the lost and bring back
the strays. I will bind up the injured and
strengthen the weak.[5]

Our Lord Jesus, that great Shepherd
of the sheep,[6] said, "I AM THE GOOD SHEP-
HERD. THE GOOD SHEPHERD LAYS DOWN HIS
LIFE FOR THE SHEEP."[7] When he saw the
crowds, he had compassion on them,
because they were harassed and helpless,
like sheep without a shepherd.[8]

You were like sheep going astray,
but now you have returned to the Shepherd and Overseer of your souls.[9]

He says, DO NOT BE AFRAID, LITTLE
FLOCK, FOR YOUR FATHER HAS BEEN
PLEASED TO GIVE YOU THE KINGDOM.[10]

*When the Chief Shepherd appears,
you will receive the crown of glory that
will never fade away.*[11]

[1]Psalm 95:7
[2]Isaiah 40:11
[3]Psalm 23:1-3
[4]Ezekiel 34:31
[5]Ezekiel 34:15,16
[6]Hebrews 13:20
[7]John 10:11
[8]Matthew 9:36
[9]1 Peter 2:25
[10]Luke 12:32
[11]1 Peter 5:4

God Is
Our Teacher

He instructs His people in the truths that they need to know.

This is what the LORD says—your Redeemer, the Holy One of Israel: "I am the LORD your God, who teaches you what is best for you, who directs you in the way you should go."[1] I will instruct you and teach you in the way you should go; I will counsel you and watch over you.[2]

God promises that *he will teach us his ways, so that we may walk in his paths.[3]* The follower of God discovers that *his God instructs him and teaches him the right way.[4]* Yes, *he will instruct him in the way chosen for him.[5]*

This was shown in Jesus who was

called *a teacher who has come from God.*[6] And when He *saw a large crowd, he had compassion on them. . .So he began teaching them many things.*[7] But *he taught as one who had authority, and not as their teachers of the law.*[8]

Jesus said that THE COUNSELOR, THE HOLY SPIRIT. . .WILL TEACH YOU ALL THINGS AND WILL REMIND YOU OF EVERYTHING I HAVE SAID TO YOU.[9] When you have to answer for your faith THE HOLY SPIRIT WILL TEACH YOU AT THAT TIME WHAT YOU SHOULD SAY.[10]

We have not received the spirit of the world but the Spirit who is from God, that we may understand what God has freely given us.[11]

Lord, since *you gave your good Spirit to instruct*[12] us, then *guide me in your truth and teach me.*[13]

Teach me to do your will, for you are my God.[14] And then may my lips overflow with praise, for you teach me your decrees.[15]

[1]Isaiah 48:17
[2]Psalm 32:8
[3]Isaiah 2:3
[4]Isaiah 28:26
[5]Psalm 25:12
[6]John 3:2
[7]Mark 6:34
[8]Matthew 7:29
[9]John 14:26
[10]Luke 12:12
[11]1 Corinthians 2:12
[12]Nehemiah 9:20
[13]Psalm 25:5
[14]Psalm 143:10
[15]Psalm 119:171

NOTES

_____

_____

_____

_____

_____

_____

_____

_____

_____

_____

_____

_____

_____

_____

_____

_____

_____

NOTES

_____

_____

_____

_____

_____

_____

_____

_____

_____

_____

_____

_____

_____

_____

_____

_____

THE
SPECIAL
ROLES
OF
JESUS

JESUS IS OUR FRIEND

He enjoys spending time with us and sharing the many things we go through.

Many years ago *Abraham believed God, and it was credited to him as righteousness, and he was called God's friend.¹* Jesus referred to this by saying, *YOUR FATHER ABRAHAM REJOICED AT THE THOUGHT OF SEEING MY DAY; HE SAW IT AND WAS GLAD.²* And when they asked Jesus how He could have known Abraham, who lived so long ago, Jesus replied, *BEFORE ABRAHAM WAS BORN, I AM!³*

People referred to Jesus as *A FRIEND OF TAX COLLECTORS AND "SINNERS."⁴* He spoke of *OUR FRIEND LAZARUS.⁵* And He called His followers *MY FRIENDS.⁶* Moreover, He told them, *GREATER LOVE HAS NO*

ONE THAN THIS, THAT ONE LAY DOWN HIS LIFE FOR HIS FRIENDS. . .I NO LONGER CALL YOU SERVANTS, BECAUSE A SERVANT DOES NOT KNOW HIS MASTER'S BUSINESS. INSTEAD, I HAVE CALLED YOU FRIENDS, FOR EVERYTHING THAT I HAVE LEARNED FROM MY FATHER I HAVE MADE KNOWN TO YOU.[7]

Jesus is *a friend who sticks closer than a brother.*[8] Truly, *a friend loves at all times.*[9] Even when He is correcting us we need to remember that *faithful are the wounds of a friend*[10] and that *the pleasantness of one's friend springs from his earnest counsel.*[11]

Jesus wants friends. Once, He saw an unpopular man viewing Him from a tree. Jesus said, *"ZACCHAEUS, COME DOWN IMMEDIATELY. I MUST STAY AT YOUR HOUSE TODAY." So he came down at once and welcomed him gladly. All the people saw this and began to mutter, "he has gone to be the guest of a 'sinner'.*"[12]

And to each of our hearts He says,
*HERE I AM! I STAND AT THE DOOR AND
KNOCK. IF ANYONE HEARS MY VOICE AND
OPENS THE DOOR, I WILL COME IN AND EAT
WITH HIM, AND HE WITH ME.*[13]

[1]James 2:23
[2]John 8:56
[3]John 8:58
[4]Matthew 11:19
[5]John 11:11
[6]Luke 12:4
[7]John 15:13,15
[8]Proverbs 18:24
[9]Proverbs 17:17
[10]Proverbs 27:6
[11]Proverbs 27:9
[12]Luke 19:5-7
[13]Revelation 3:20

Jesus Is Our Interceding Priest

He goes before the judgment seat as the Righteous One, to plead our case with His Father, the Judge.

Christ Jesus, who died—more than that, who was raised to life—is at the right hand of God and is also interceding for us.[1] To satisfy justice *he bore the sin of many, and made intercession for the transgressors.*[2]

And now *he is able to save completely those who come to God through him, because he always lives to intercede for them.*[3]

Jesus showed this when He promised His followers, *I WILL ASK THE FATHER, AND HE WILL GIVE YOU ANOTHER*

COUNSELOR TO BE WITH YOU FOREVER— THE SPIRIT OF TRUTH.[4]

When Simon Peter was facing temptation, Jesus told him, *I HAVE PRAYED FOR YOU, SIMON, THAT YOUR FAITH MAY NOT FAIL.*[5]

To His Father He said, *MY PRAYER IS NOT THAT YOU TAKE THEM OUT OF THE WORLD BUT THAT YOU PROTECT THEM FROM THE EVIL ONE. . .SANCTIFY THEM BY THE TRUTH; YOUR WORD IS TRUTH.*[6]

Finally, on the cross He prayed, *FATHER, FORGIVE THEM, FOR THEY DO NOT KNOW WHAT THEY ARE DOING.*[7]

Since we have a great high priest who has gone through the heavens, Jesus the Son of God, let us hold firmly to the faith we profess. For we do not have a high priest who is unable to sympathize with our weaknesses, but we have one who has been tempted in every way, just as we are—yet was without sin.[8]

If anybody does sin, we have one who speaks to the Father in our defense —Jesus Christ, the Righteous One.[9]

[1]Romans 8:34
[2]Isaiah 53:12
[3]Hebrews 7:25
[4]John 14:16
[5]Luke 22:32
[6]John 17:15,17
[7]Luke 23:34
[8]Hebrews 4:14,15
[9]1 John 2:1

JESUS IS
OUR MEDIATOR

Being fully God and fully human, Jesus is the perfect communication link to bring God and people together.

Jesus, the mediator of a new covenant, [1] said, *I AM GOD'S SON.* [2] At one time *a voice from heaven said, "This is My Son."* [3] Jesus is also *THE SON OF MAN.* [4] He even stated, *THE SON OF GOD. . .IS THE SON OF MAN.* [5]

For us *there is one God and one mediator between God and men, the man Christ Jesus.* [6] *Who as to his human nature was a descendant of David, and who through the Spirit of holiness was declared with power to be the Son of God by his resurrection from the dead: Jesus Christ our Lord.* [7]

Yes, Jesus can relate to people and to God. So now *Christ is the mediator of a new covenant, that those who are called may receive the promised eternal inheritance—now that he has died as a ransom to set them free.*[8]

When we were God's enemies, we were reconciled to him through the death of his Son.[9] *And now, since we have been justified through faith, we have peace with God through our Lord Jesus Christ.*[10]

In him and through faith in him we may approach God with freedom and confidence.[11]

God was reconciling the world to himself in Christ, not counting men's sins against them. . .We are therefore Christ's ambassadors, as though God were making his appeal through us. We implore you on Christ's behalf: Be reconciled to God.[12]

[1]Hebrews 12:24
[2]John 10:36
[3]Matthew 3:17
[4]Matthew 16:13
[5]John 5:25,27
[6]1 Timothy 2:5
[7]Romans 1:3,4
[8]Hebrews 9:15
[9]Romans 5:10
[10]Romans 5:1
[11]Ephesians 3:12
[12]2 Corinthians 5:19,20

JESUS IS OUR MESSIAH/CHRIST

He is specially appointed to overcome the world, the flesh, and the Devil.

Peter said, *you are the Christ, the Son of the living God.[1]* Another said, *"I know that Messiah" (called Christ) "is coming. When he comes, he will explain everything to us." Then Jesus declared, "I WHO SPEAK TO YOU AM HE."[2]*

Jesus' judge said, *"I charge you under oath by the living God: Tell us if you are the Christ* (or Messiah), *the Son of God. "YES, IT IS AS YOU SAY," JESUS REPLIED. "BUT I SAY TO YOU: IN THE FUTURE YOU WILL SEE THE SON OF MAN SITTING AT THE RIGHT HAND OF THE MIGHTY ONE AND COMING ON THE CLOUDS OF HEAVEN."[3]*

Yes, *Jesus is the Christ* (or Messiah).*

People can trust Him since *he too shared in their humanity, so that by his death he might destroy him who holds the power of death—that is, the devil—and free those who all their lives were held in slavery by their fear of death.*[5]

And then *God exalted him to the highest place and gave him the name that is above every name, that at the name of Jesus every knee should bow, in heaven and on earth and under the earth, and every tongue confess that Jesus Christ is Lord, to the glory of God the Father.*[6]

You see, the Scriptures *are written that you may believe that Jesus is the Christ, the Son of God, and that by believing you may have life in his name.*[7] *Because everyone who believes that Jesus is the Christ is born of God.*[8]

This is the victory that has overcome the world, even our faith.[9] For this faith is in Jesus who says, *I HAVE TOLD YOU THESE THINGS, SO THAT IN ME YOU MAY HAVE PEACE. IN THIS WORLD YOU WILL HAVE TROUBLE. BUT TAKE HEART! I HAVE OVERCOME THE WORLD.*[10]

[1]Matthew 16:16
[2]John 4:25,26
[3]Matthew 26:63,64
[4]Acts 9:22
[5]Hebrews 2:14,15
[6]Philippians 2:9-11
[7]John 20:31
[8]1 John 5:1
[9]1 John 5:4
[10]John 16:33

JESUS IS OUR REDEEMER

He comes on behalf of ones who are sold into the hands of this world and "buys" them back for Himself.

Our Redeemer—the LORD Almighty is his name—is the Holy One.[1] He is our great God and Savior, Jesus Christ, who gave himself for us to redeem us from all wickedness and to purify for himself a people that are his very own, eager to do what is good.[2]

The redemption that came by Christ Jesus[3] purchased men for God from every tribe and language and people and nation.[4] God sent his Son. . .to redeem those under law, that we might receive the full rights of sons.[5]

Christ redeemed us from the curse (penalty) of the law by becoming a curse for us. . .he redeemed us in order that the blessing given to Abraham might come to the Gentiles through Christ Jesus, so that by faith we might receive the promise of the Spirit.[6]

Yes, *the Redeemer will come. . .to those who repent of their sins.*[7] And then we have *redemption, the forgiveness of sins.*[8]

Remember, *you were redeemed from the empty way of life handed down to you from your forefathers. . . with the precious blood of Christ.*[9] He is *your Redeemer, who formed you in the womb.*[10] And now *you are not your own; you were bought at a price. Therefore honor God with your body.*[11]

Fear not, for I have redeemed you; I

have called you by name; you are Mine.[12]
"I myself will help you," declares the
LORD, your Redeemer.[13]

[1]Isaiah 47:4
[2]Titus 2:13,14
[3]Romans 3:24
[4]Revelation 5:9
[5]Galatians 4:4,5
[6]Galatians 3:13,14
[7]Isaiah 59:20
[8]Colossians 1:14
[9]1 Peter 1:18,19
[10]Isaiah 44:24
[11]1 Corinthians 6:19,20
[12]Isaiah 43:1
[13]Isaiah 41:14

Jesus Is
Our Savior

He rescues us from the eternal judgment against our sins and from the everyday pain that wrong living brings.

We have seen and testify that the Father has sent his Son to be the Savior of the world.[1] The fact is, God did not appoint us to wrath but to receive salvation through our Lord Jesus Christ.[2]

Salvation is found in no one else, for there is no other name under heaven given to men by which we must be saved.[3]

It comes from *our Savior, Christ Jesus, who has destroyed death and has brought life and immortality to light through the gospel.[4] For Christ Jesus* came into the world to save sinners.[5]

GOD DID NOT SEND HIS SON INTO THE WORLD TO CONDEMN THE WORLD, BUT TO SAVE THE WORLD THROUGH HIM.[6] Yes, THE SON OF MAN CAME TO SEEK AND TO SAVE WHAT WAS LOST.[7]

God exalted him to his own right hand as Prince and Savior, that he might give repentance and forgiveness of sins.[8]

Because of this, he is able to save completely those who come to God through him.[9]

God says, Turn to me and be saved, all you ends of the earth; for I am God, and there is no other.[10] And Jesus says, I AM THE GATE; WHOEVER ENTERS THROUGH ME WILL BE SAVED.[11]

So now, if you confess with your

mouth, "Jesus is Lord," and believe in your heart that God raised him from the dead, you will be saved.[12] Because everyone who calls on the name of the Lord will be saved.[13]

[1] John 4:14
[2] 1 Thessalonians 5:9
[3] Acts 4:12
[4] 2 Timothy 1:10
[5] 1 Timothy 1:15
[6] John 3:17
[7] Luke 19:10
[8] Acts 5:31
[9] Hebrews 7:25
[10] Isaiah 45:22
[11] John 10:9
[12] Romans 10:9
[13] Romans 10:13

JESUS IS OUR SUBSTITUTE SACRIFICE

Even though He was innocent of all sin, He took on the sin of the world and its punishment, to clear us of guilt.

God made him who had no sin to be sin for us, so that in him we might become the righteousness of God.¹ he loved us and sent his Son as an atoning sacrifice for our sins.² This was the Lord Jesus Christ, who gave himself for our sins to rescue us from the present evil age, according to the will of our God and Father.³

In fact, *he appeared so that he might take away our sins. And in him is no sin,⁴* because He is *Jesus Christ, the Righteous One. He is the atoning sacrifice for our sins, and not only for ours but also for the sins of the whole world.[5]*

In other words, *he suffered death, so that by the grace of God he might taste death for everyone.[6]*

Yes, *Christ died for sins once for all, the righteous for the unrighteous, to bring you to God. He was put to death in the body but made alive by the Spirit.[7]*

Just as man is destined to die once, and after that to face judgment, so Christ was sacrificed once to take away the sins of many people; and he will appear a second time, not to bear sin, but to bring salvation to those who are waiting for him.[8]

He was chosen before the creation of the world, but was revealed in these last times for your sake. Through him you believe in God, who raised him from the dead and glorified him, and so your faith and hope are in God.[9] Therefore, we have this hope as an anchor for the soul, firm and secure.[10]

[1]2 Corinthians 5:21
[2]1 John 4:10
[3]Galatians 1:3,4
[4]1 John 3:5
[5]1 John 2:1,2
[6]Hebrews 2:9
[7]1 Peter 3:18
[8]Hebrews 9:27,28
[9]1 Peter 1:20,21
[10]Hebrews 6:19

NAMES THAT PICTURE JESUS

Bread of life—*I AM THE BREAD OF LIFE. HE WHO COMES TO ME WILL NEVER GO HUNGRY, AND HE WHO BELIEVES IN ME WILL NEVER BE THIRSTY. . .IF A MAN EATS OF THIS BREAD, HE WILL LIVE FOREVER.*[1]

Cornerstone—*Christ Jesus himself as the chief cornerstone.*[2] *A chosen and precious cornerstone, and the one who trusts in him will never be put to shame.*[3]

First and Last—*DO NOT BE AFRAID. I AM THE FIRST AND THE LAST. I AM THE LIVING ONE; I WAS DEAD, AND BEHOLD I AM ALIVE FOR EVER AND EVER! AND I HOLD THE KEYS OF DEATH AND HADES.*[4]

Gate—*I AM THE GATE FOR THE SHEEP . . .I AM THE GATE; WHOEVER ENTERS*

THROUGH ME WILL BE SAVED.[5]

Head—*Christ is the head of the church, his body, of which he is the Savior.*[6] *he is the head of the body, the church.*[7]

King—*On his robe and on his thigh he has this name written: KING OF KINGS AND LORD OF LORDS.*[8] *Jesus Christ . . .the ruler of the kings of the earth.*[9]

Life—*I AM. . .THE LIFE.*[10] *I AM THE RESURRECTION AND THE LIFE. HE WHO BELIEVES IN ME WILL LIVE, EVEN THOUGH HE DIES.*[11]

Light—*I AM THE LIGHT OF THE WORLD. WHOEVER FOLLOWS ME WILL NEVER WALK IN DARKNESS, BUT WILL HAVE THE LIGHT OF LIFE.*[12] *I HAVE COME INTO THE WORLD AS A LIGHT, SO THAT NO ONE WHO BELIEVES IN ME SHOULD STAY IN DARKNESS.*[13]

Prophet—*This is Jesus, the prophet from Nazareth in Galilee.*[14] *I must keep going* (to Jerusalem). . .*FOR SURELY NO PROPHET CAN DIE OUTSIDE JERUSALEM!*[15]

Rock—*They drank from the spiritual rock that accompanied them, and that rock was Christ.*[16] *I lay in Zion a stone that causes men to stumble and a rock that makes them fall, and the one who trusts in him will never be put to shame.*[17]

Vine—*I am the true vine. . .I am the vine; you are the branches. If a man remains in me and I in him, he will bear much fruit; apart from me you can do nothing.*[18]

Way—*I AM THE WAY. . .NO ONE COMES TO THE FATHER EXCEPT THROUGH ME.*[19] *WE HAVE CONFIDENCE TO ENTER THE MOST HOLY PLACE BY THE BLOOD OF JESUS, BY A*

NEW AND LIVING WAY OPENED FOR US.[20]

Witness—*Jesus Christ, who is the faithful witness.*[21] *FOR THIS REASON I WAS BORN, AND FOR THIS I CAME INTO THE WORLD, TO TESTIFY TO THE TRUTH. EVERYONE ON THE SIDE OF TRUTH LISTENS TO ME.*[22]

Word—*In the beginning was the Word, and the Word was with God, and the Word was God. . .The Word became flesh and made his dwelling among us.*[23] *And his name is the Word of God.*[24]

[1]John 6:35,51
[2]Ephesians 2:20
[3]1 Peter 2:6
[4]Revelation 1:17,18
[5]John 10:7,9
[6]Ephesians 5:23
[7]Colossians 1:18

[8]Revelation 19:16
[9]Revelation 1:5
[10]John 14:6
[11]John 11:25
[12]John 8:12
[13]John 12:46
[14]Matthew 21:11
[15]Luke 13:33
[16]1 Corinthians 10:4
[17]Romans 9:33
[18]John 15:1,5
[19]John 14:6
[20]Hebrews 10:19
[21]Revelation 1:5
[22]John 18:37
[23]John 1:1,14
[24]Revelation 19:13

SPECIAL ROLES
OF THE HOLY SPIRIT

He acknowledges Christ—*WHEN THE COUNSELOR COMES, WHOM I WILL SEND TO YOU FROM THE FATHER, THE SPIRIT OF TRUTH WHO GOES OUT FROM THE FATHER, HE WILL TESTIFY ABOUT ME.[1] HE WILL BRING GLORY TO ME BY TAKING FROM WHAT IS MINE AND MAKING IT KNOWN TO YOU.[2]*

He comforts and counsels—*I WILL ASK THE FATHER, AND HE WILL GIVE YOU ANOTHER COUNSELOR TO BE WITH YOU FOR-EVER—THE SPIRIT OF TRUTH.[3] The church throughout Judea, Galilee and Samaria enjoyed a time of peace. It was strength-ened and encouraged by the Holy Spirit.[4]*

He convinces us of our need—*HE WILL CONVICT THE WORLD OF GUILT IN*

REGARD TO SIN AND RIGHTEOUSNESS AND JUDGMENT: IN REGARD TO SIN, BECAUSE MEN DO NOT BELIEVE IN ME; IN REGARD TO RIGHTEOUSNESS, BECAUSE I AM GOING TO THE FATHER, WHERE YOU CAN SEE ME NO LONGER; AND IN REGARD TO JUDGMENT, BECAUSE THE PRINCE OF THIS WORLD NOW STANDS CONDEMNED.[5]

He creates new life—*FLESH GIVES BIRTH TO FLESH, BUT THE SPIRIT GIVES BIRTH TO SPIRIT.*[6] *he saved us through the washing of rebirth and renewal by the Holy Spirit.*[7]

He grants special knowledge—*HE WILL TELL YOU WHAT IS YET TO COME.*[8] *Prophecy never had its origin in the will of man, but men spoke from God as they were carried along by the Holy Spirit.*[9]

He grows spiritual fruit—*The fruit of the Spirit is love, joy, peace, patience,*

kindness, goodness, faithfulness, gentleness and self-control.[10]

He helps us pray—*The Spirit helps
us in our weakness. We do not know
what we ought to pray, but the Spirit
himself intercedes for us with groans
that words cannot express.[11] Pray in the
Spirit on all occasions with all kinds of
prayers and requests.[12]*

He imparts truth—*THE COUNSELOR,
THE HOLY SPIRIT, WHOM THE FATHER WILL
SEND IN MY NAME, WILL TEACH YOU ALL
THINGS AND WILL REMIND YOU OF EVERY-
THING I HAVE SAID TO YOU.[13] WHEN HE, THE
SPIRIT OF TRUTH, COMES, HE WILL GUIDE
YOU INTO ALL TRUTH.[14]*

He inspires God's word—*The
Scripture had to be fulfilled which the
Holy Spirit spoke long ago.[15] All Scrip-
ture is God-breathed.[16]*

He leads God's children—*Those who are led by the Spirit of God are sons of God.*[17] *Live by the Spirit, and you will not gratify the desires of the sinful nature. . .If you are led by the Spirit, you are not under the law.*[18]

He proves our adoption by God—*The Spirit himself testifies with our spirit that we are God's children.*[19] *We know that we live in him and he in us, because he has given us of his Spirit.*[20]

He seals us for heaven—*Having believed, you were marked in him with a seal, the promised Holy Spirit, who is a deposit guaranteeing our inheritance until the redemption of those who are God's possession.*[21]

He sends forth messengers—*The Spirit said to him, "Simon, three men are looking for you. So get up and go down-*

stairs. *Do not hesitate to go with them.*"[22] *The Holy Spirit said, "Set apart for me Barnabas and Saul for the work to which I have called them". . .The two of them, sent on their way by the Holy Spirit. . . when they arrived at Salamis, they proclaimed the word of God.*[23]

He supplies wise words—*DO NOT WORRY ABOUT HOW YOU WILL DEFEND YOUR-SELVES OR WHAT YOU WILL SAY, FOR THE HOLY SPIRIT WILL TEACH YOU AT THAT TIME WHAT YOU SHOULD SAY.*[24] *This is what we speak, not in words taught us by human wisdom but in words taught by the Spirit, expressing spiritual truths in spiritual words.*[25]

[1]John 15:26
[2]John 16:14
[3]John 14:16,17
[4]Acts 9:31

[5]John 16:8-11
[6]John 3:6
[7]Titus 3:5
[8]John 16:13
[9]2 Peter 1:21
[10]Galatians 5:22-23
[11]Romans 8:26
[12]Ephesians 6:18
[13]John 14:26
[14]John 16:13
[15]Acts 1:16
[16]2 Timothy 3:16
[17]Romans 8:14
[18]Galatians 5:16,18
[19]Romans 8:16
[20]1 John 4:13
[21]Ephesians 1:13,14
[22]Acts 10:19,20
[23]Acts 13:2,4,5
[24]Luke 12:11,12
[25]1 Corinthians 2:13

NOTES

_____

_____

_____

_____

_____

_____

_____

_____

_____

_____

_____

_____

_____

_____

_____

Inspirational Library

Beautiful purse/pocket size editions of Christian classics bound in flexible leatherette. These books make thoughtful gifts for everyone on your list, including yourself!

The Bible Promise Book Over 1000 promises from God's Word arranged by topic. What does God promise about matters like: Anger, Illness, Jealousy, Love, Money, Old Age, and Mercy? Find out in this book!
>   Flexible Leatherette $3.97

Daily Light One of the most popular daily devotionals with readings for both morning and evening.
>   Flexible Leatherette $4.97

Wisdom from the Bible Daily thoughts from Proverbs which communicate truths about ourselves and the world around us.
>   Flexible Leatherette $4.97

My Daily Prayer Journal Each page is dated and features a Scripture verse and ample room for you to record your thoughts, prayers, and praises. One page for each day of the year.
>   Flexible Leatherette $4.97

Available wherever books are sold.
Or order from:

Barbour & Company, Inc.
P.O. Box 719
Uhrichsville, OH 44683
http://www.barbourbooks.com

If you order by mail add $2.00 to your order for shipping.
Prices subject to change without notice.